CANDY BARCHIVE

A VISUAL ARCHIVE OF AMERICA'S FAVORITE CANDY

KIRA STACKHOUSE

NUENA

ABOUT

Candy Barchive is a visual archive and tribute to the candy we all know and love. This book includes everyday candybars and packaged candies that are found in grocery and convenience stores across the country, wrapped up and cross-sectioned for your visual enjoyment.

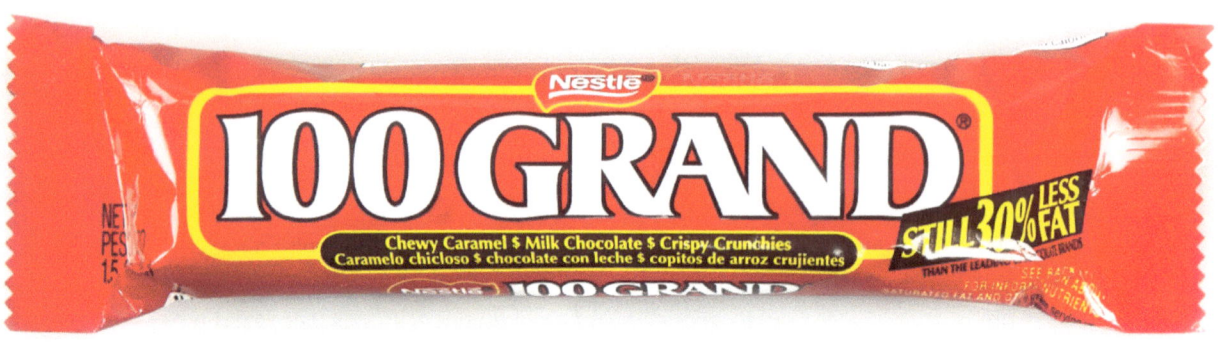

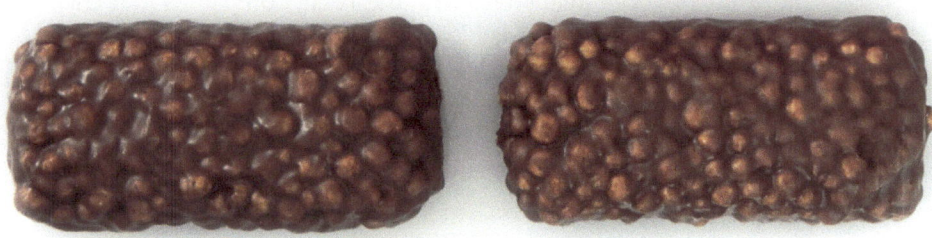

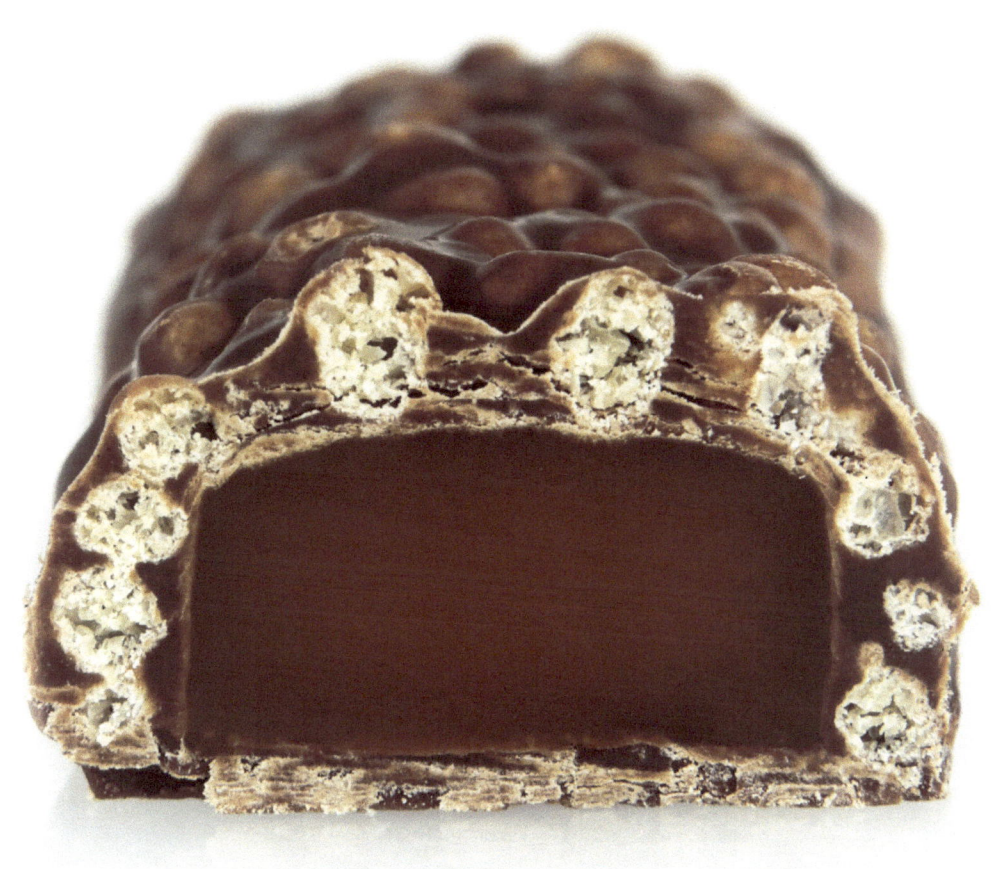

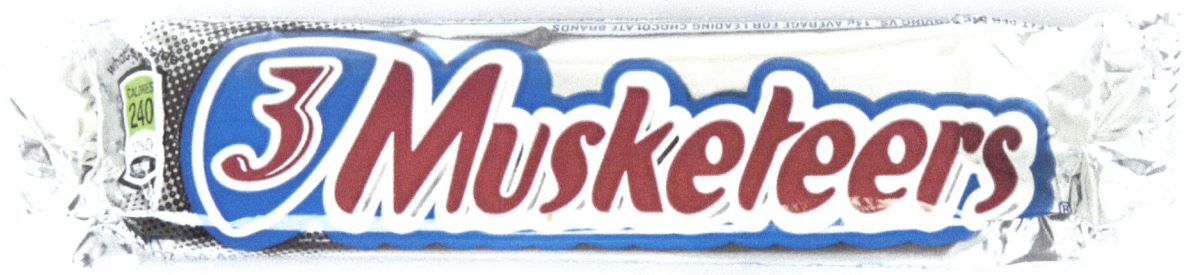

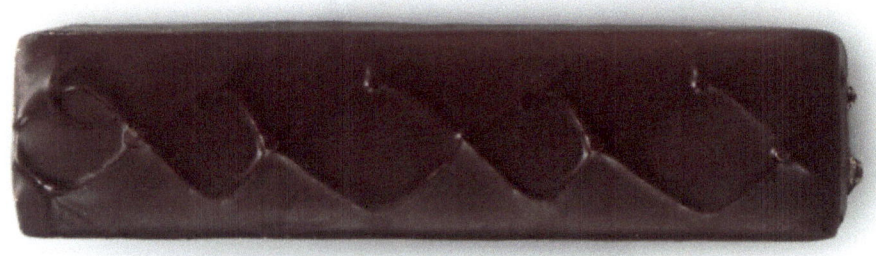

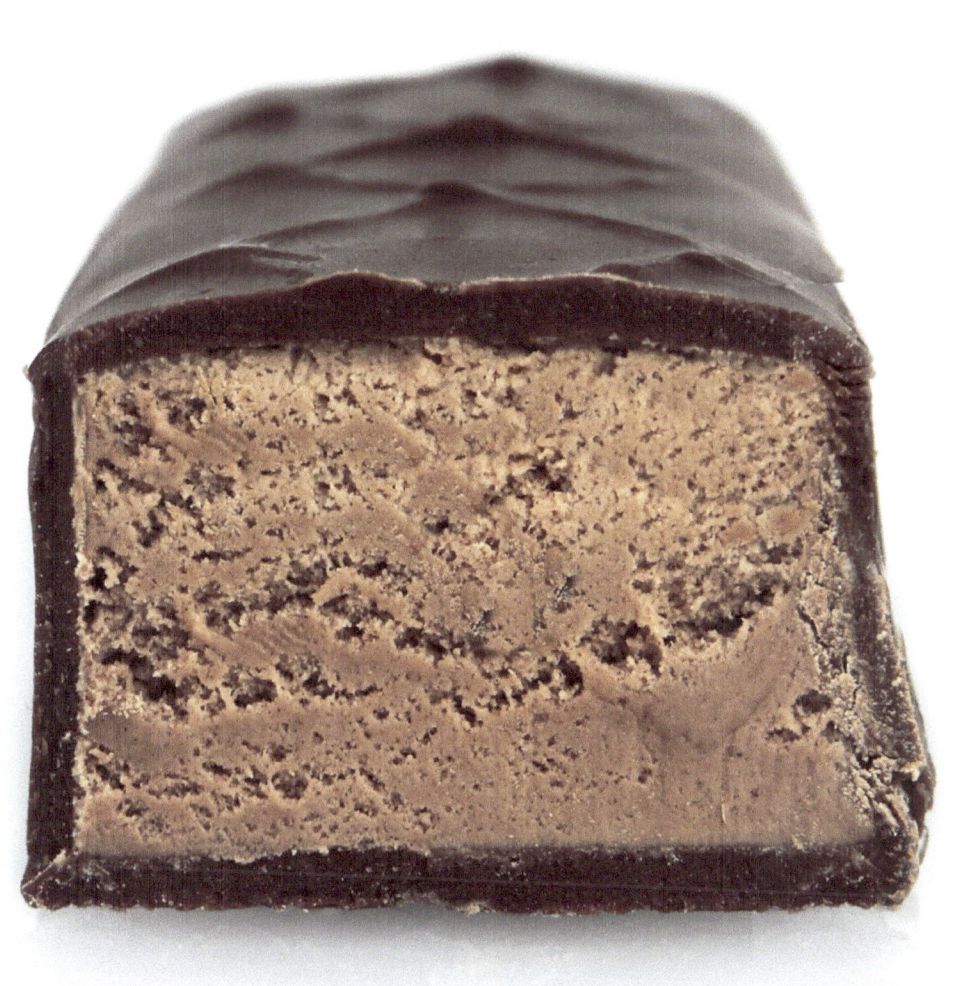

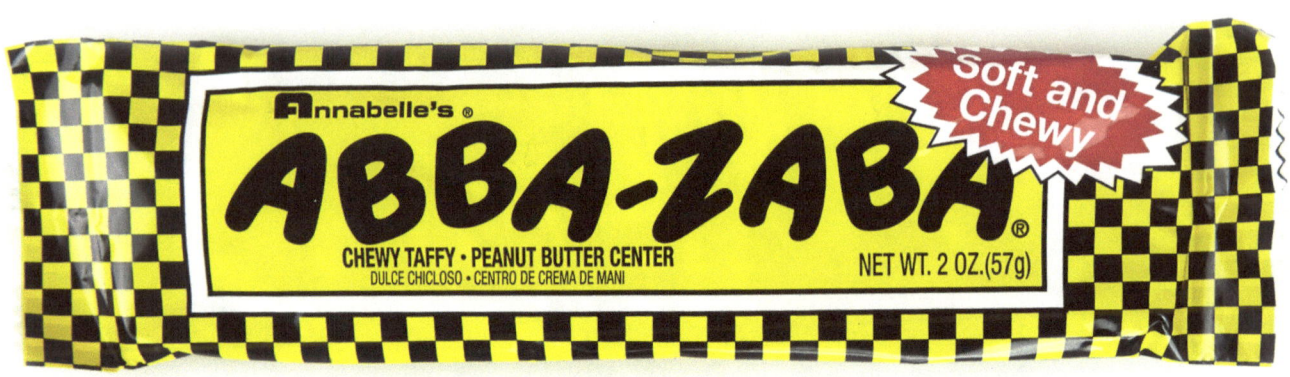

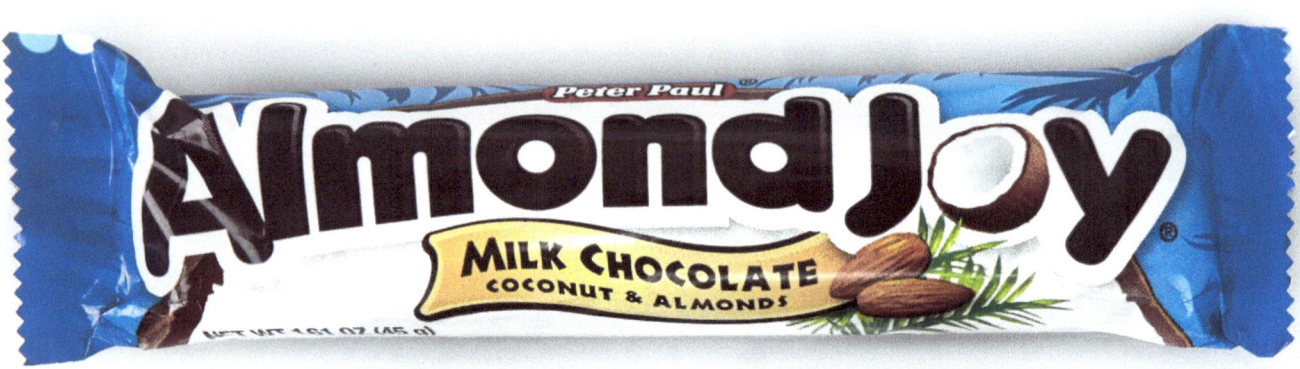

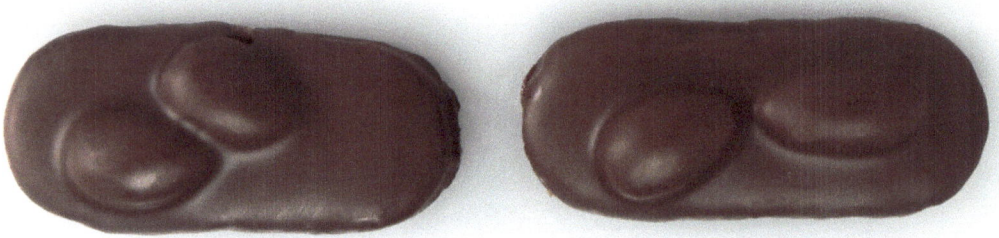

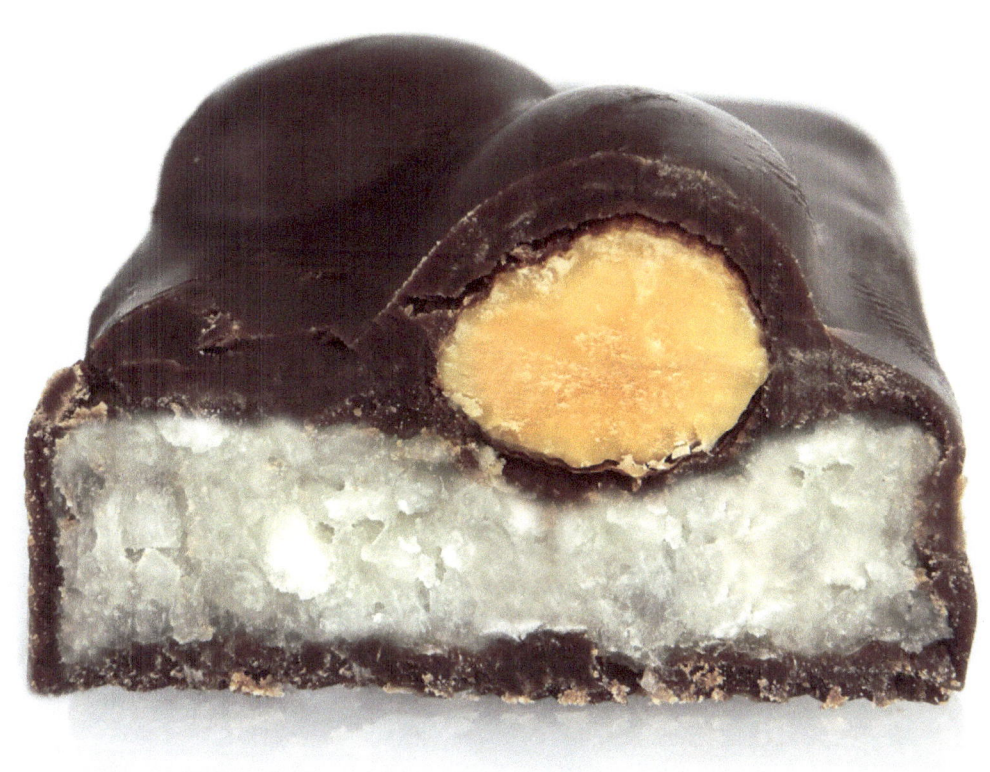

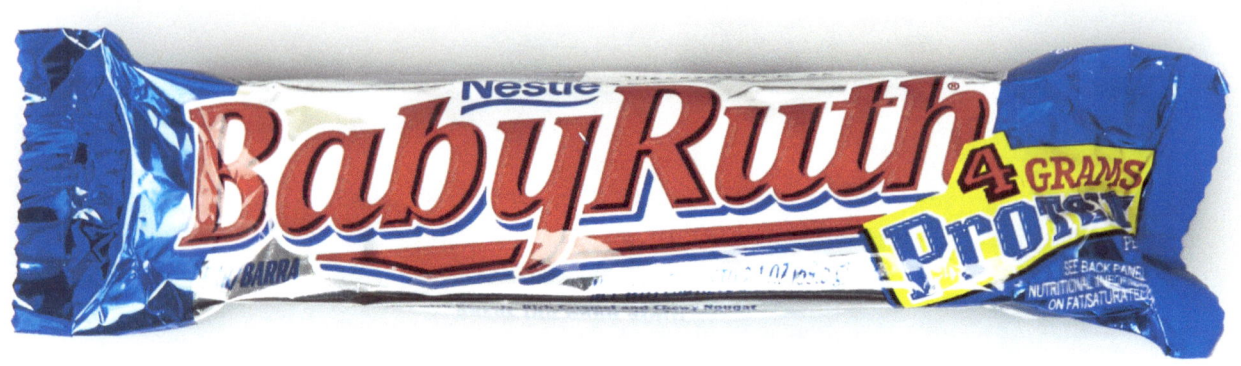

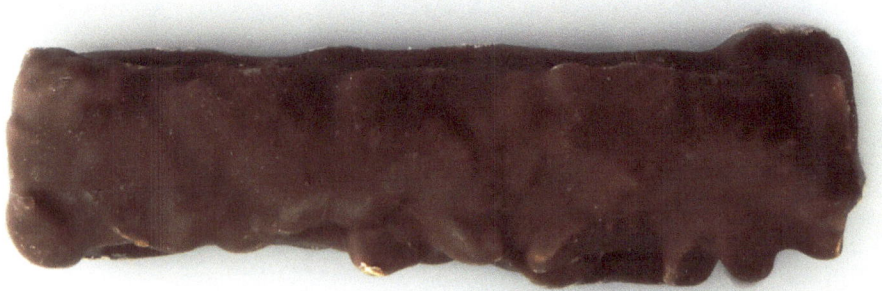

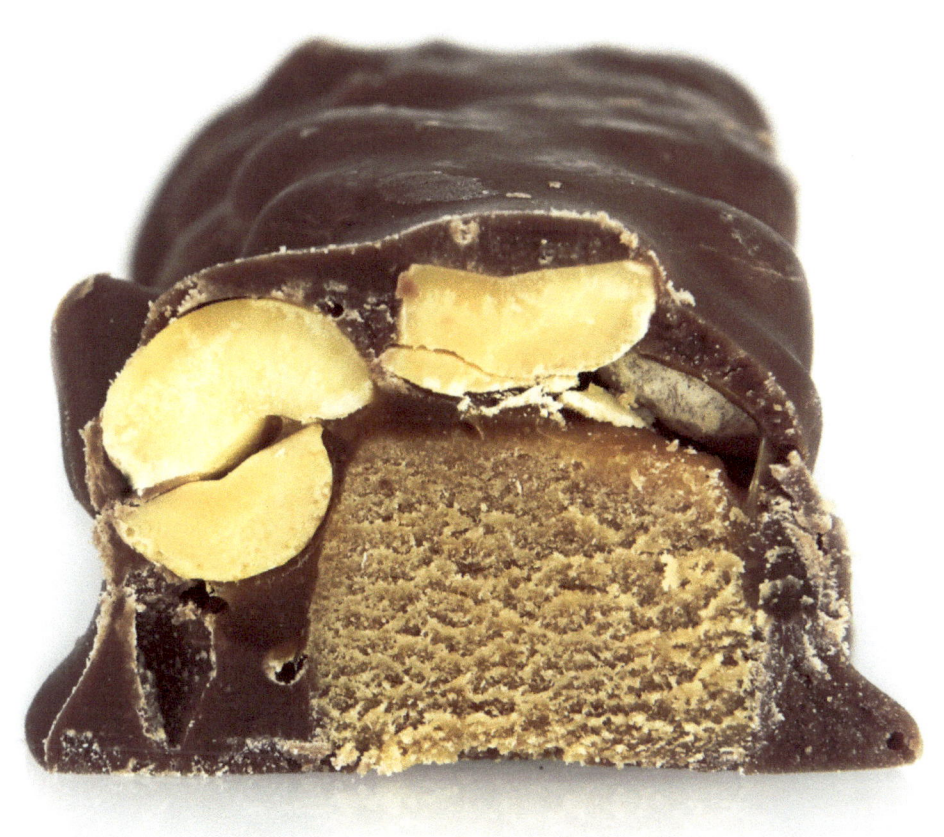

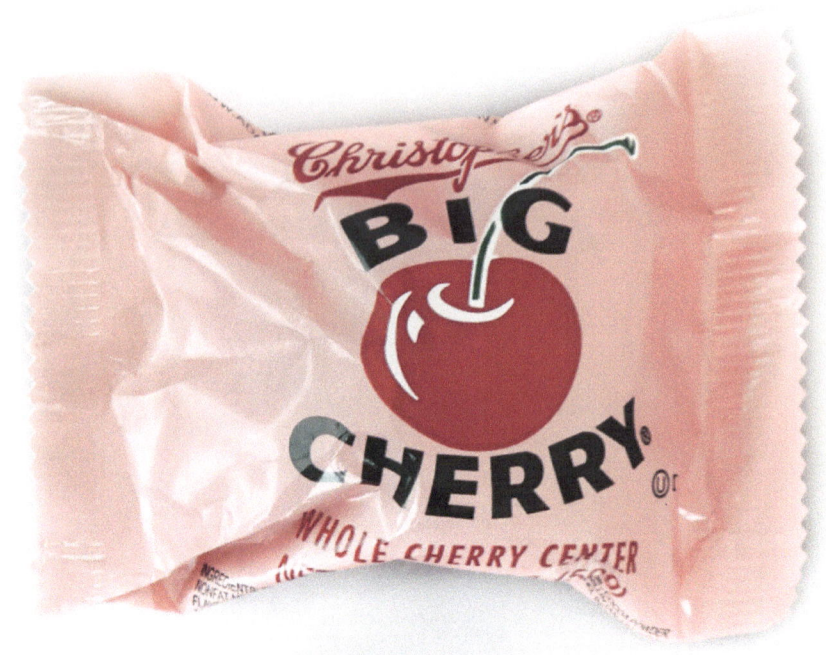

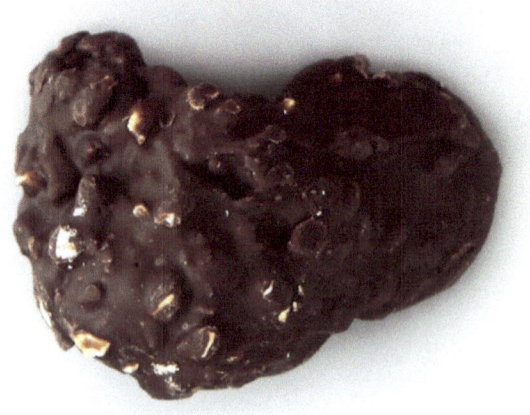

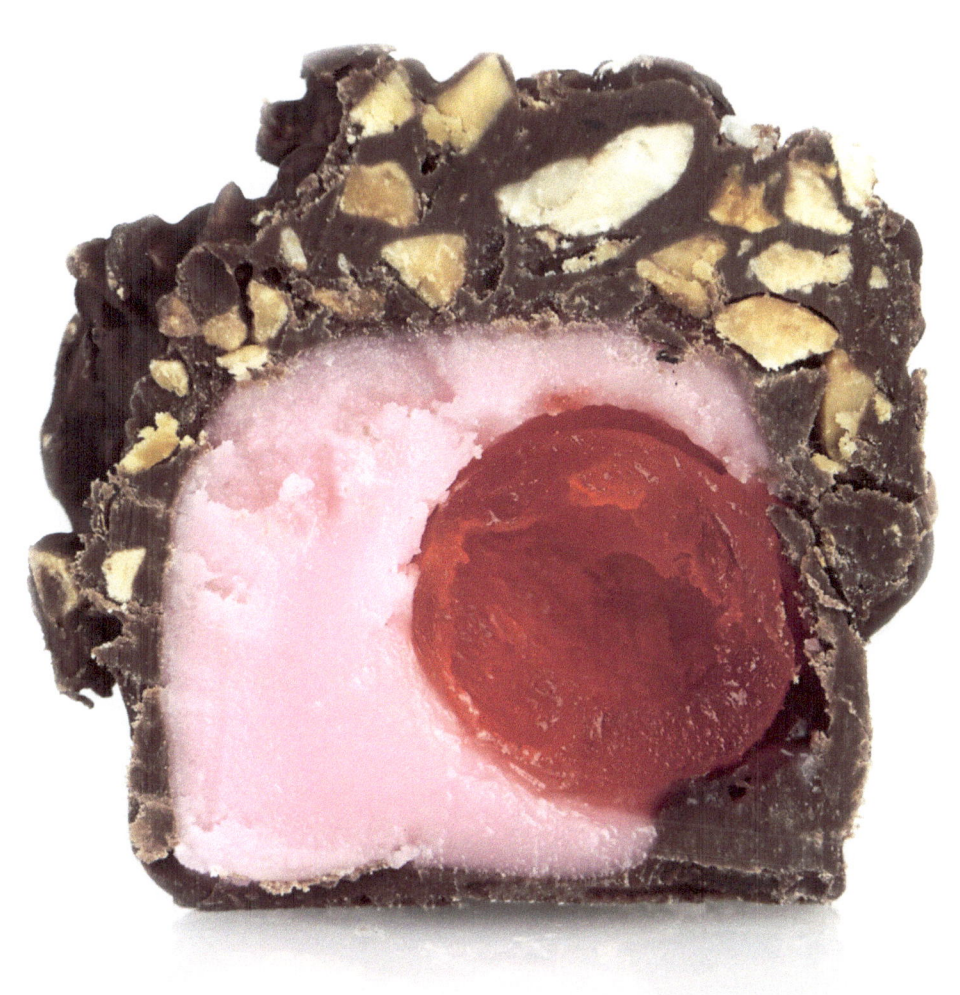

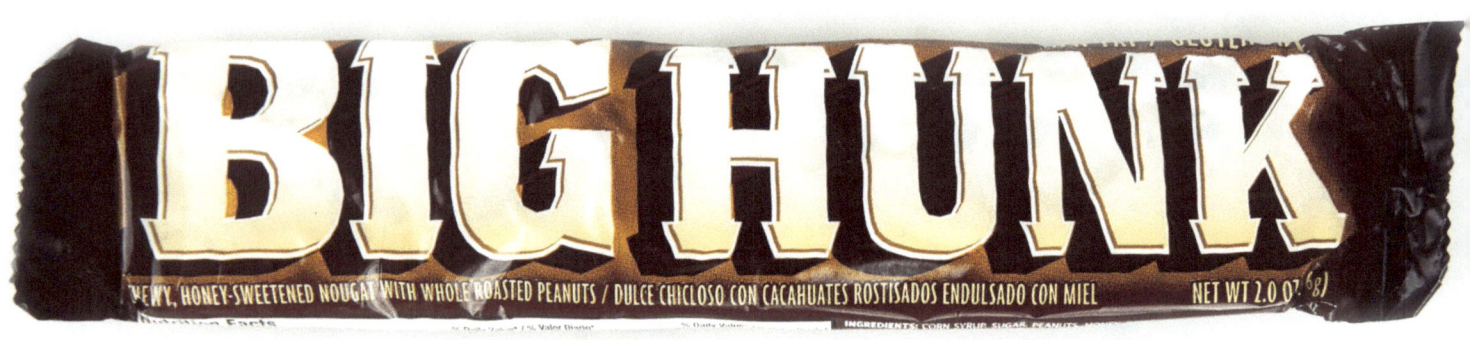

CHEWY, HONEY-SWEETENED NOUGAT WITH WHOLE ROASTED PEANUTS / DULCE CHICLOSO CON CACAHUATES ROSTISADOS ENDULSADO CON MIEL   NET WT 2.0 OZ (6g)

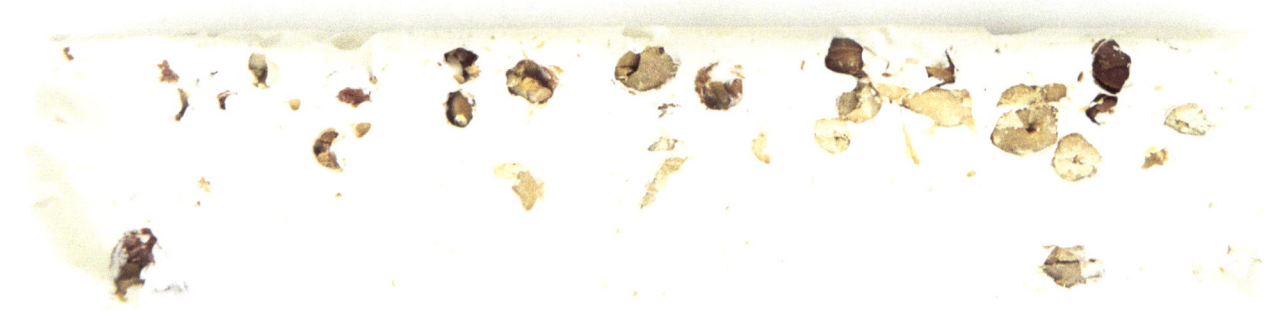

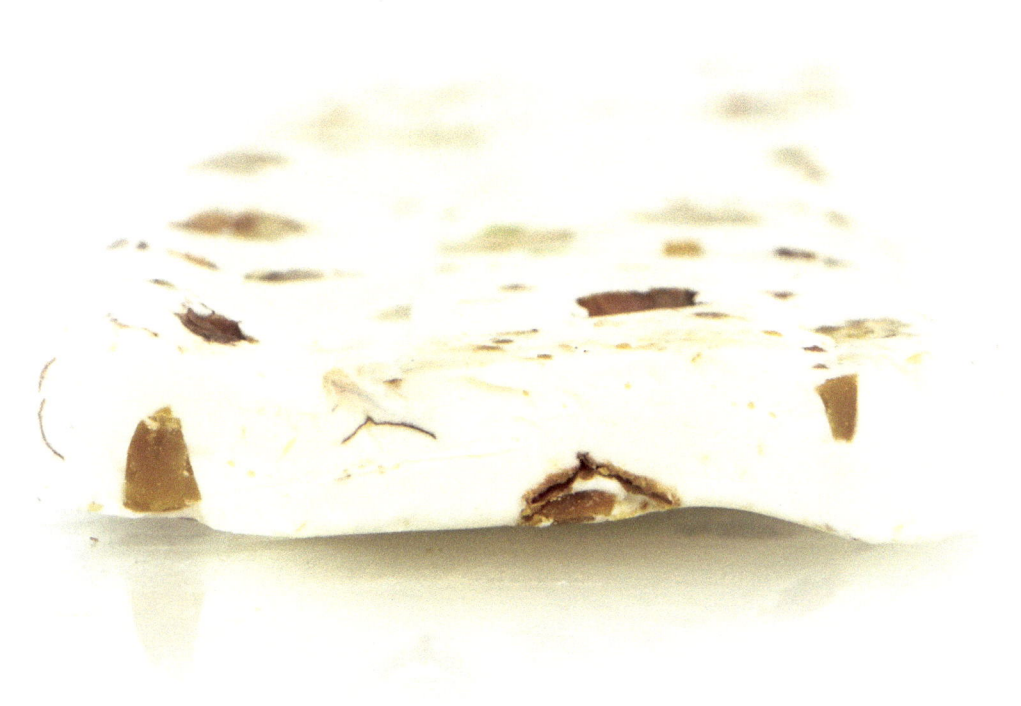

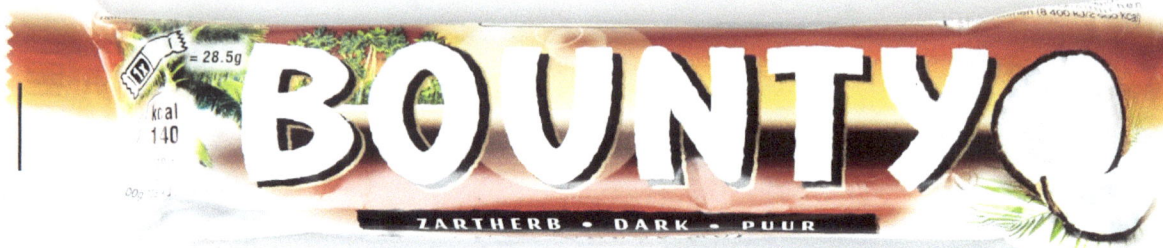

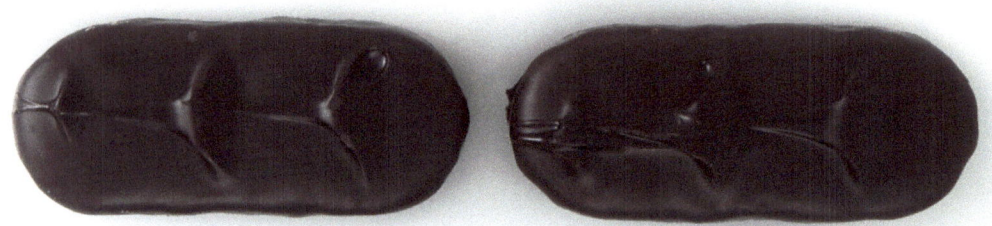

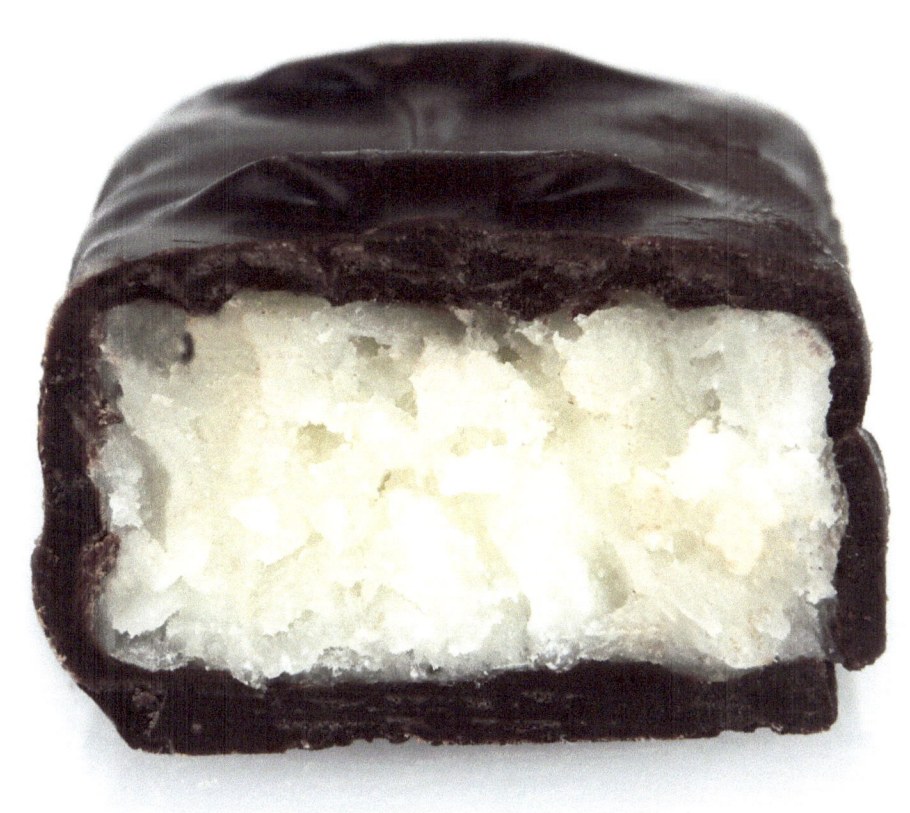

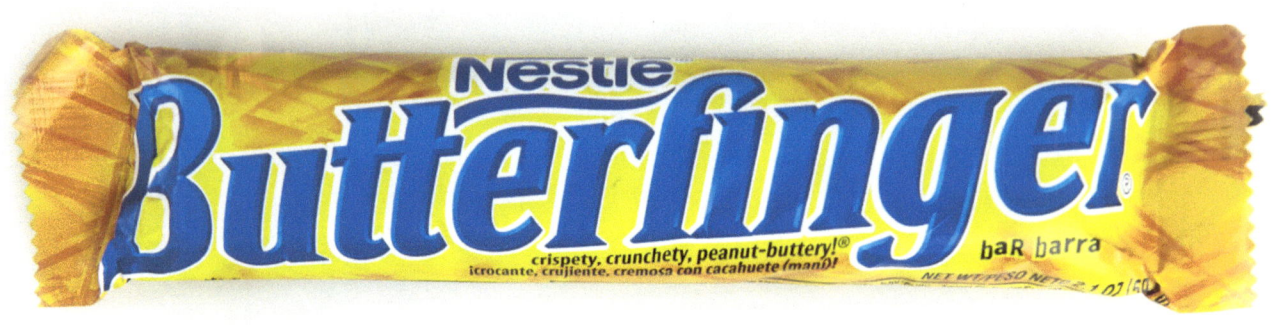

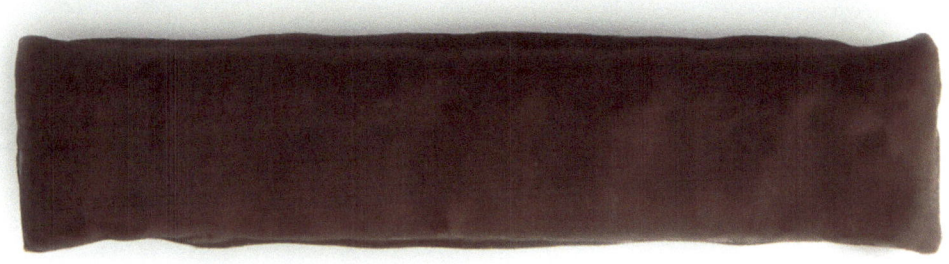

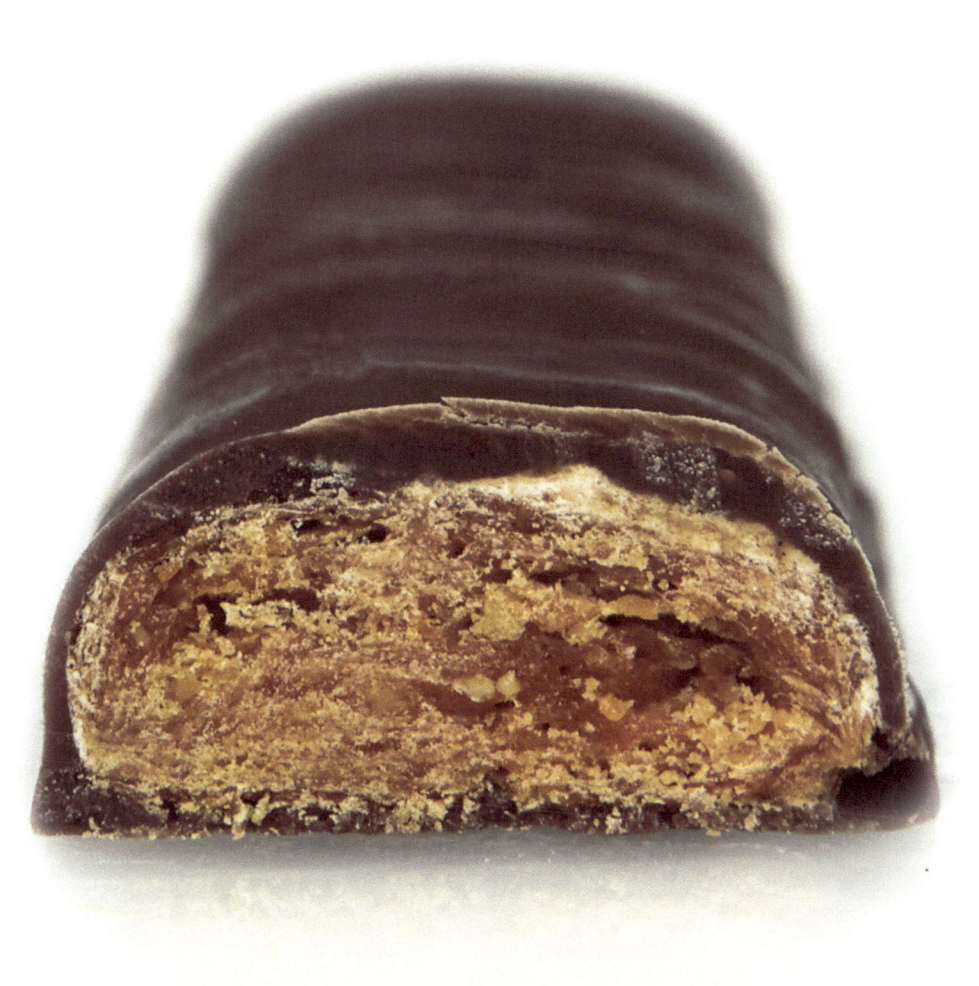

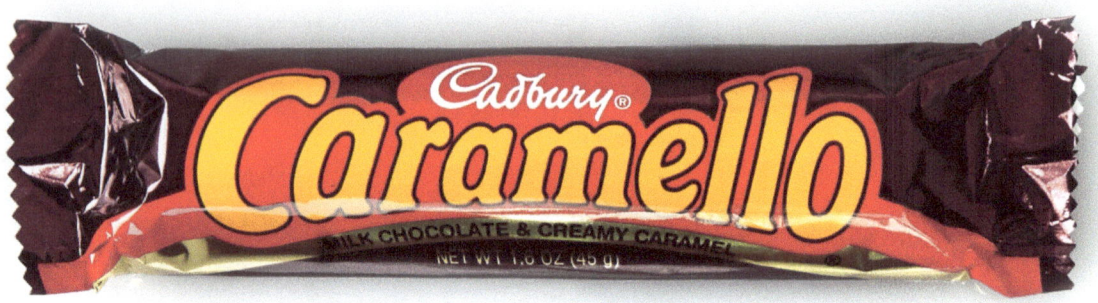

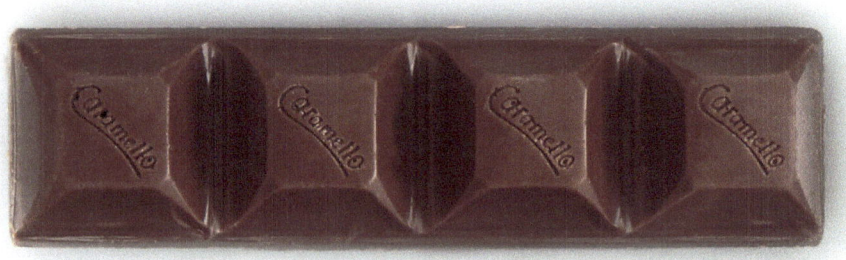

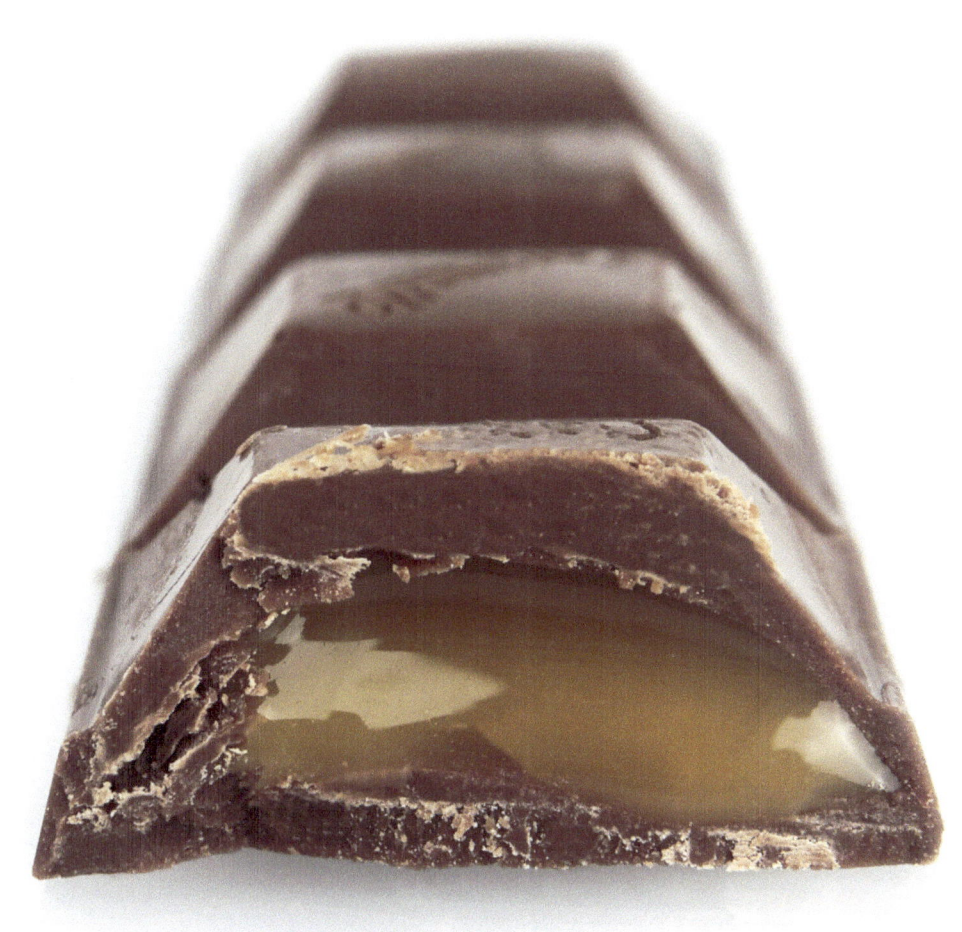

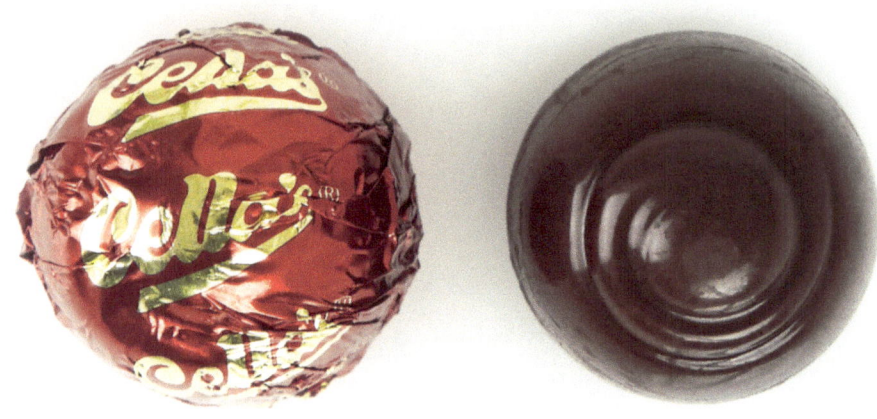

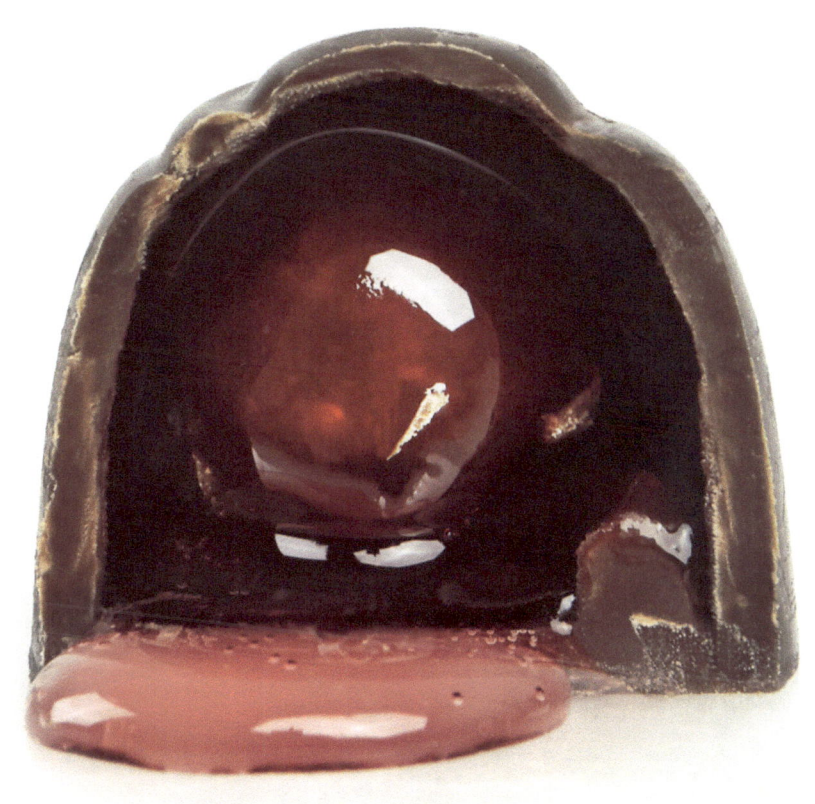

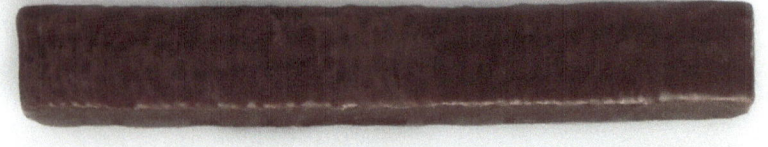

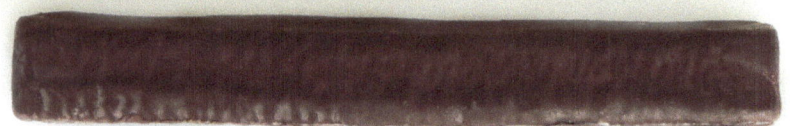

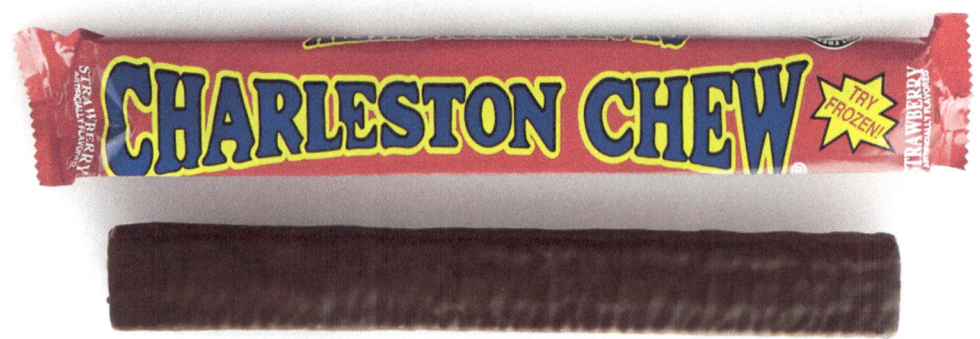

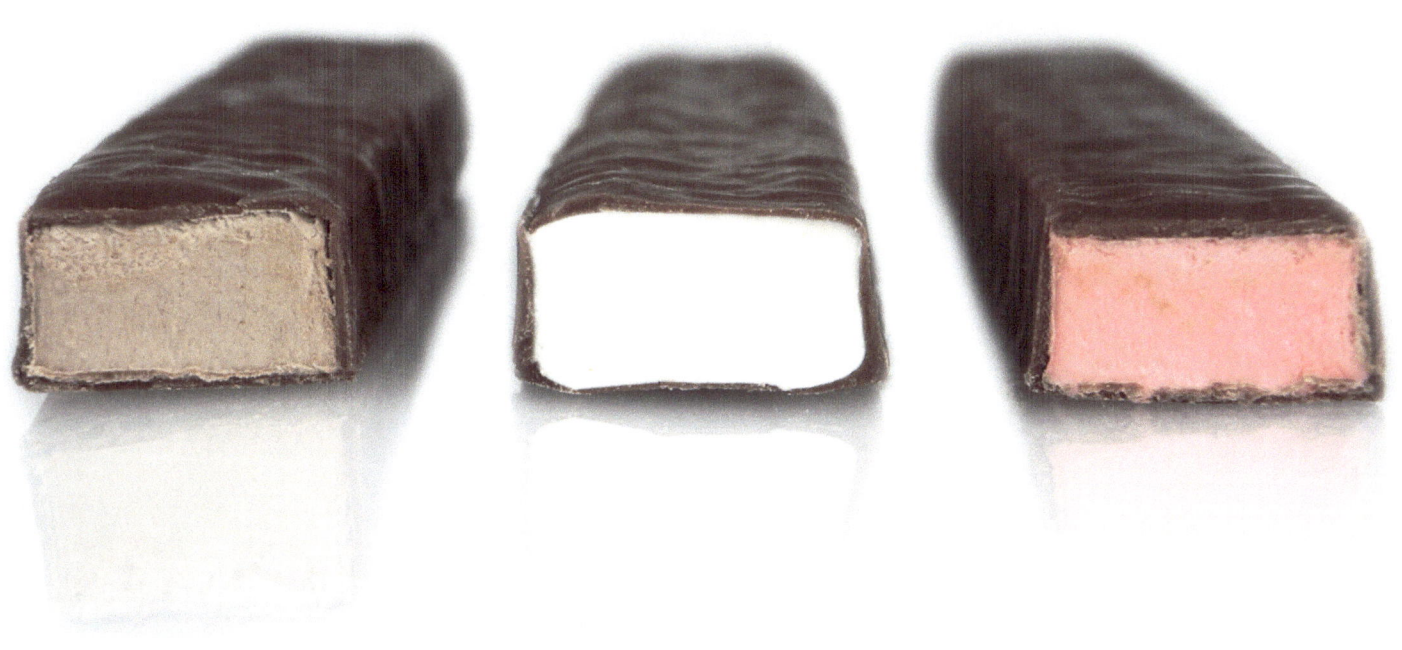

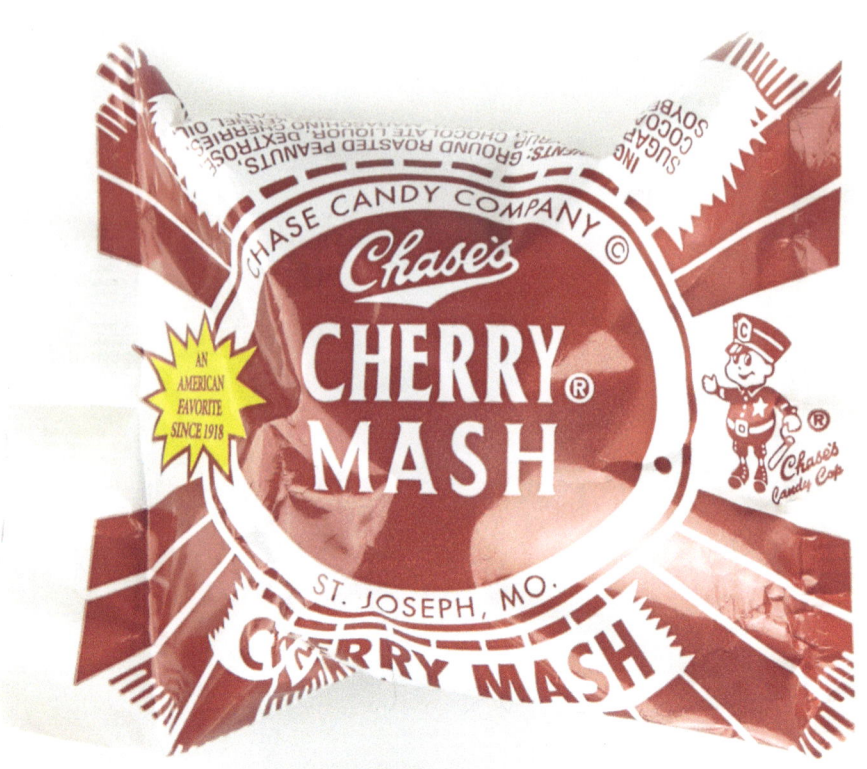

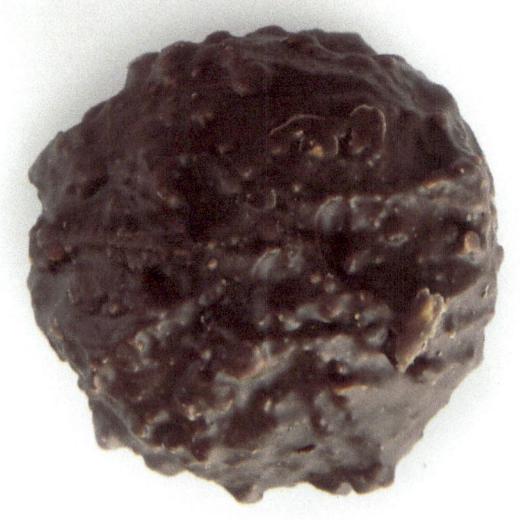

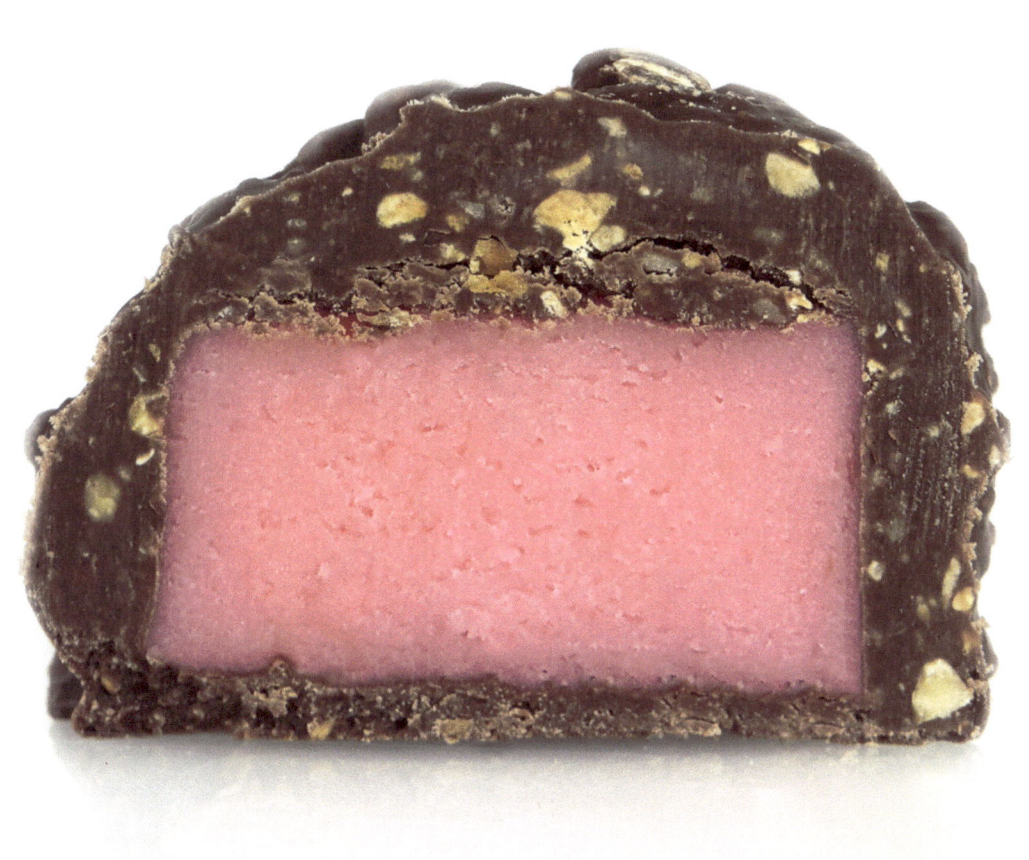

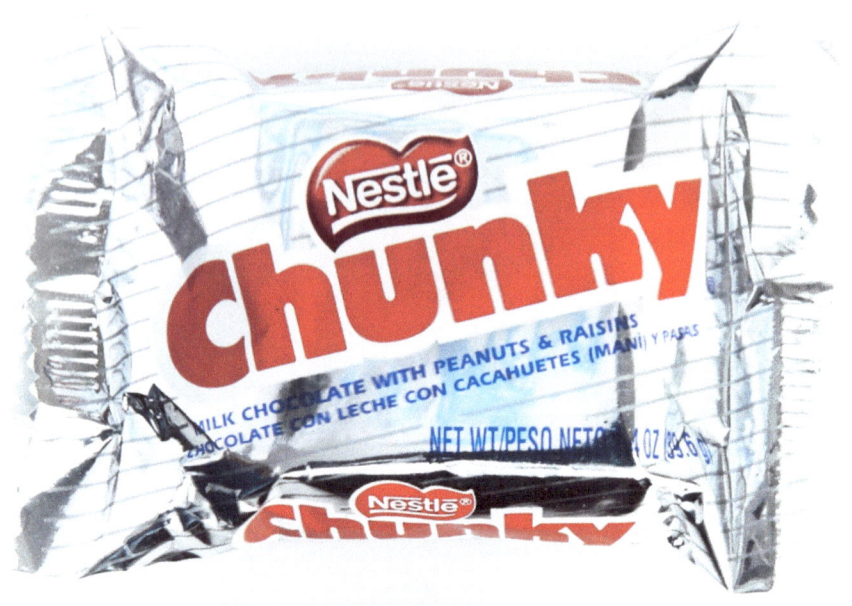

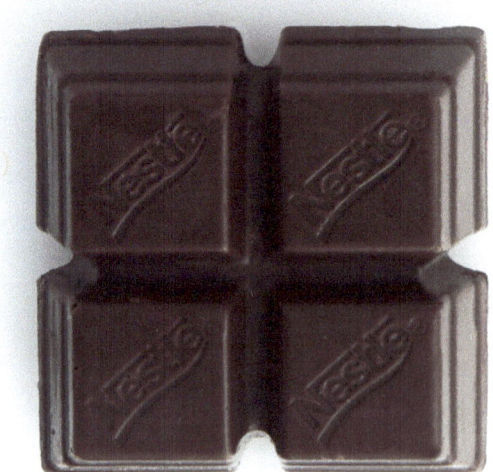

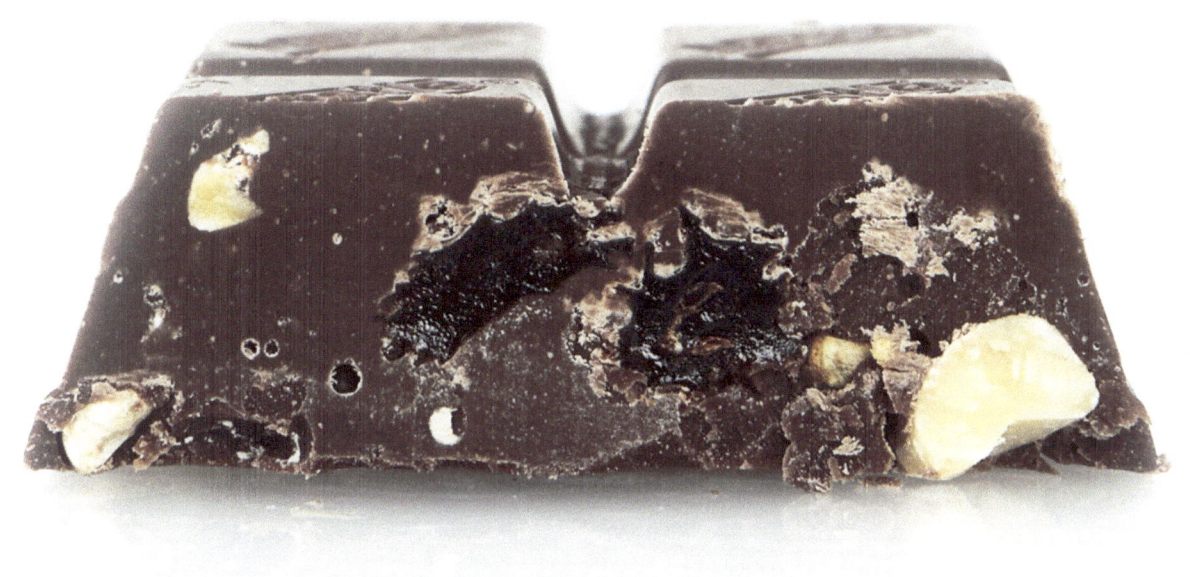

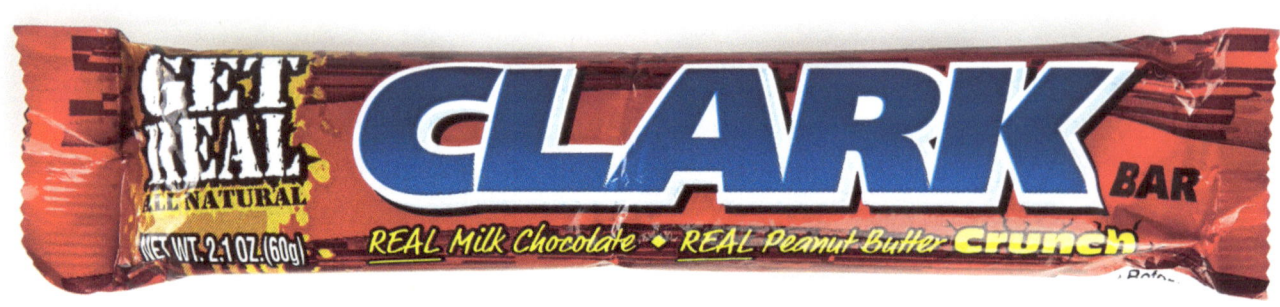

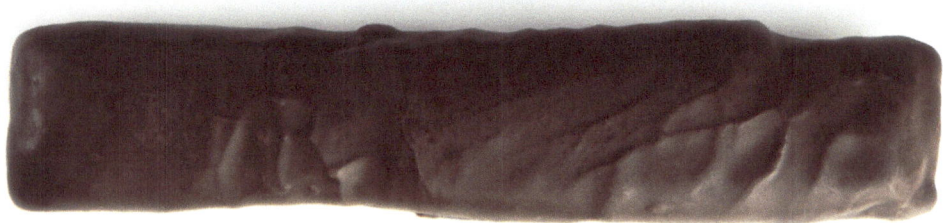

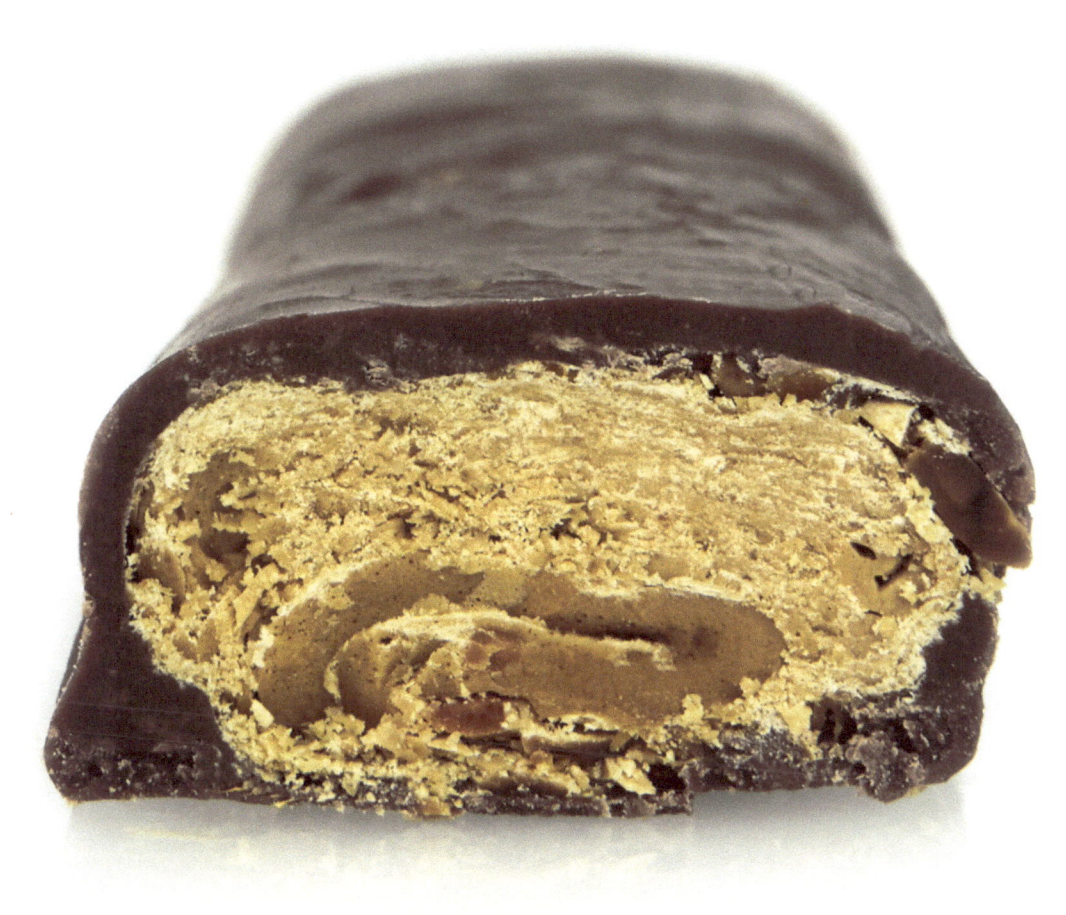

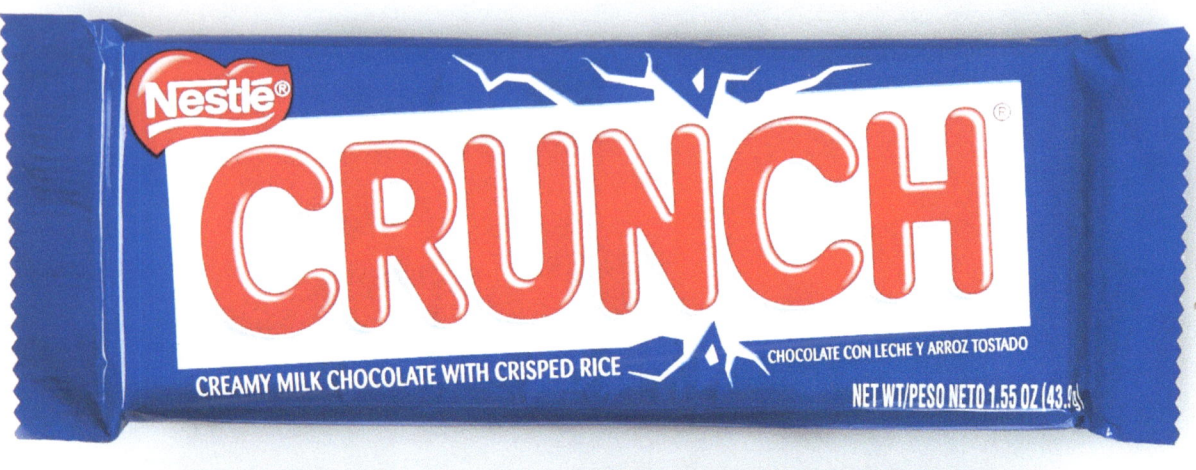

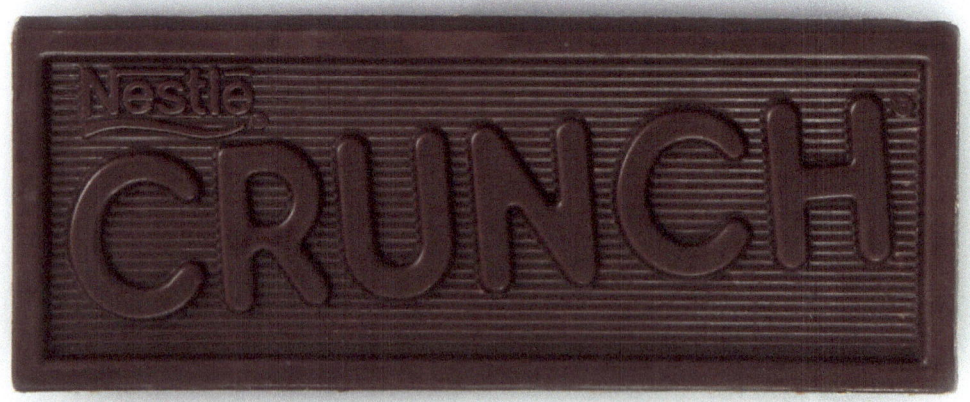

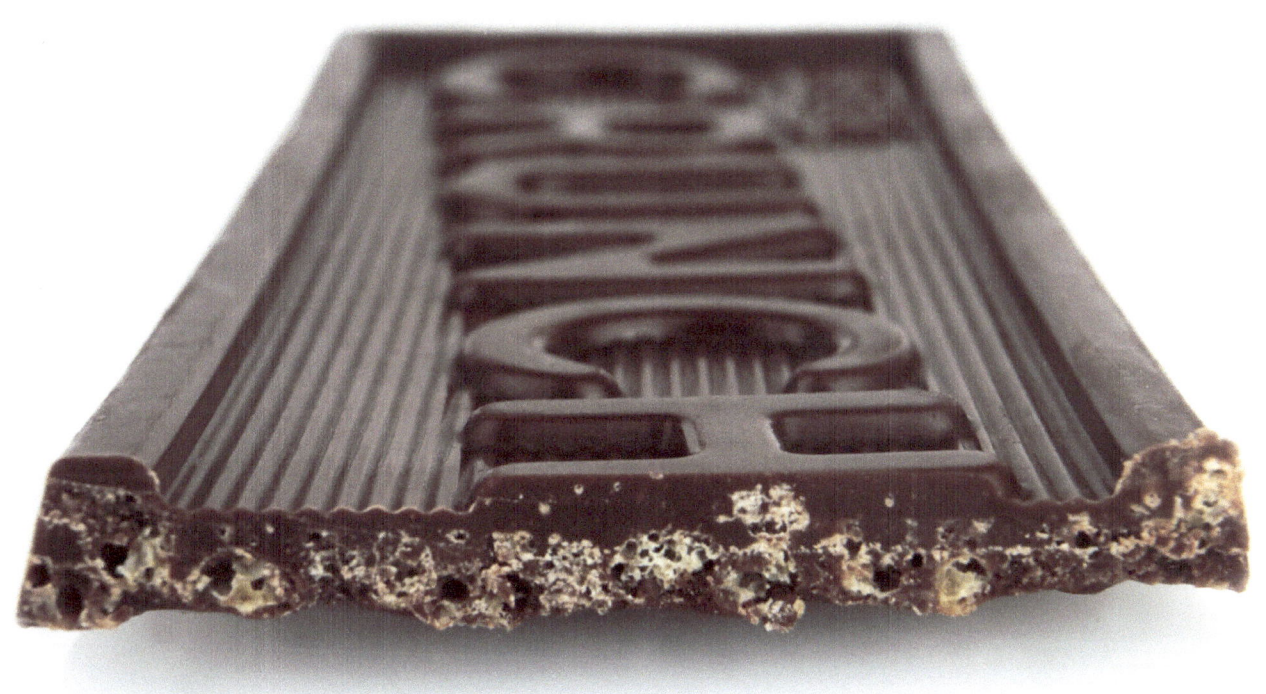

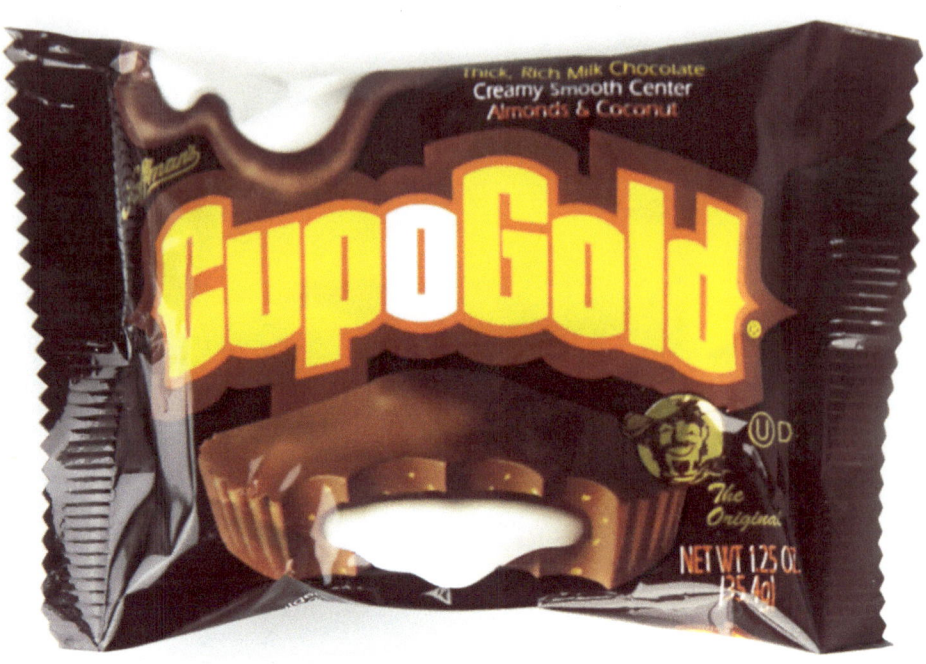

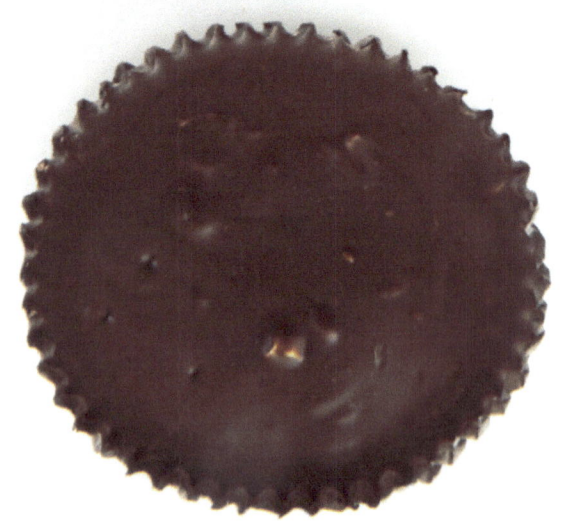

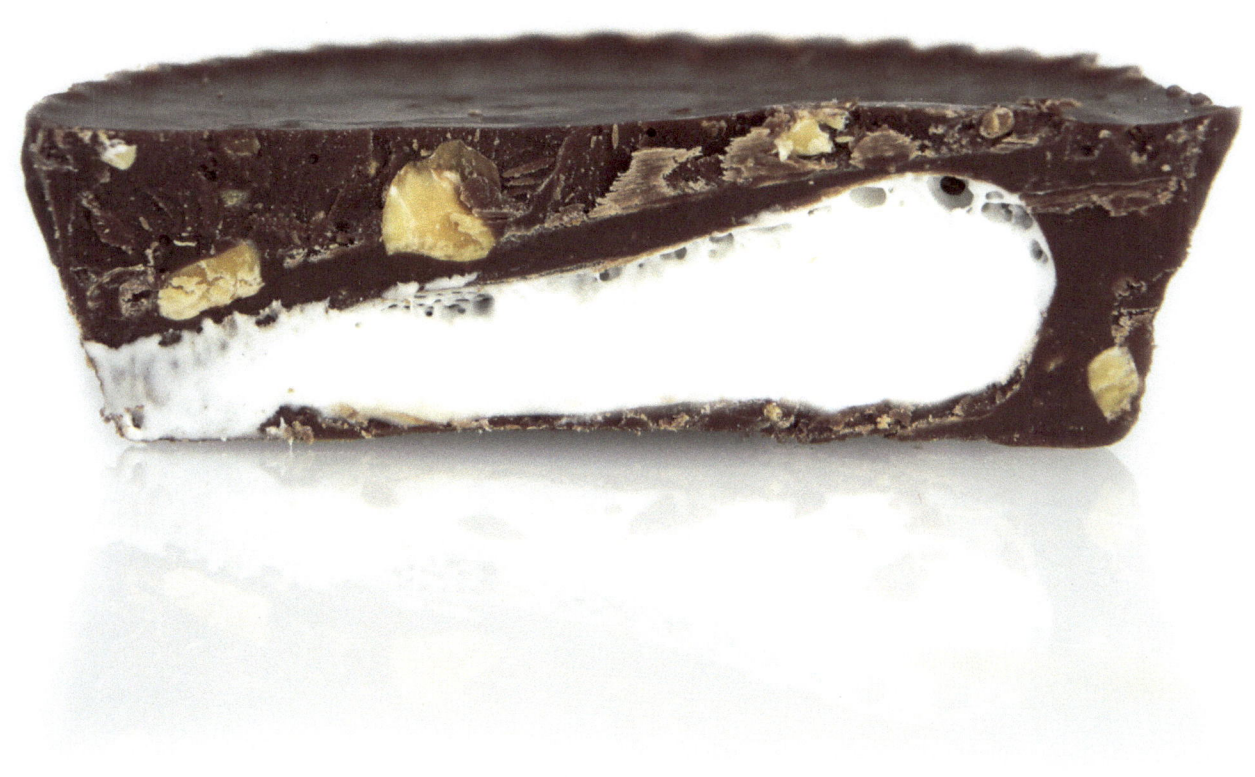

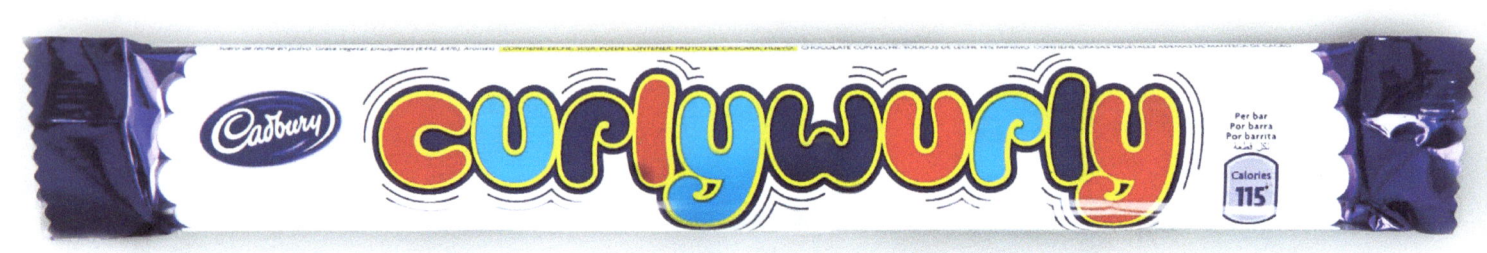

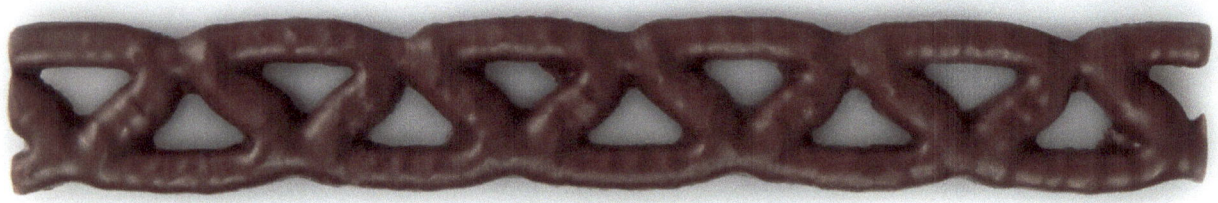

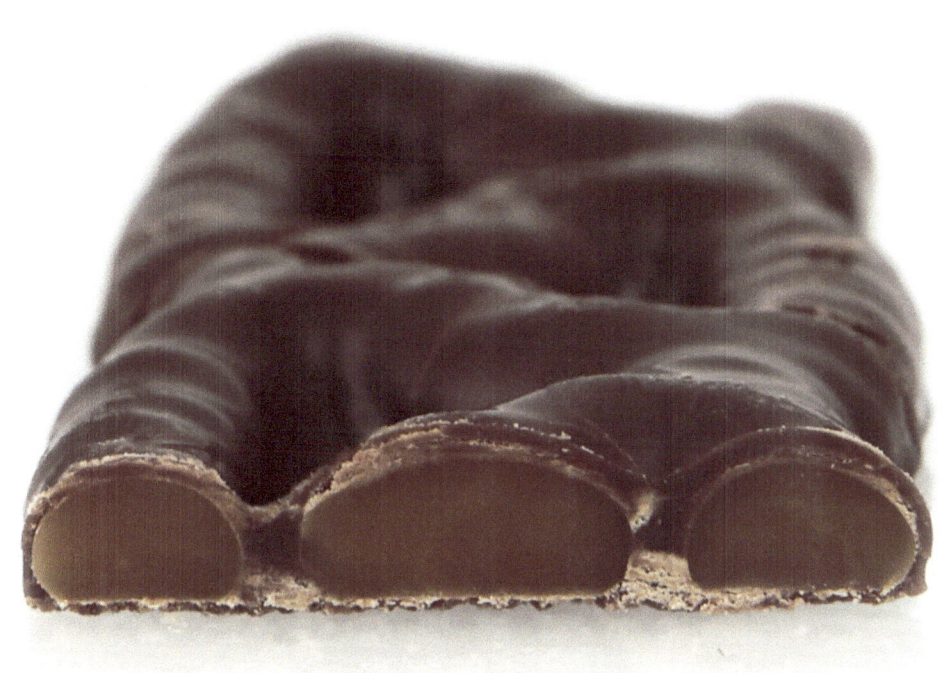

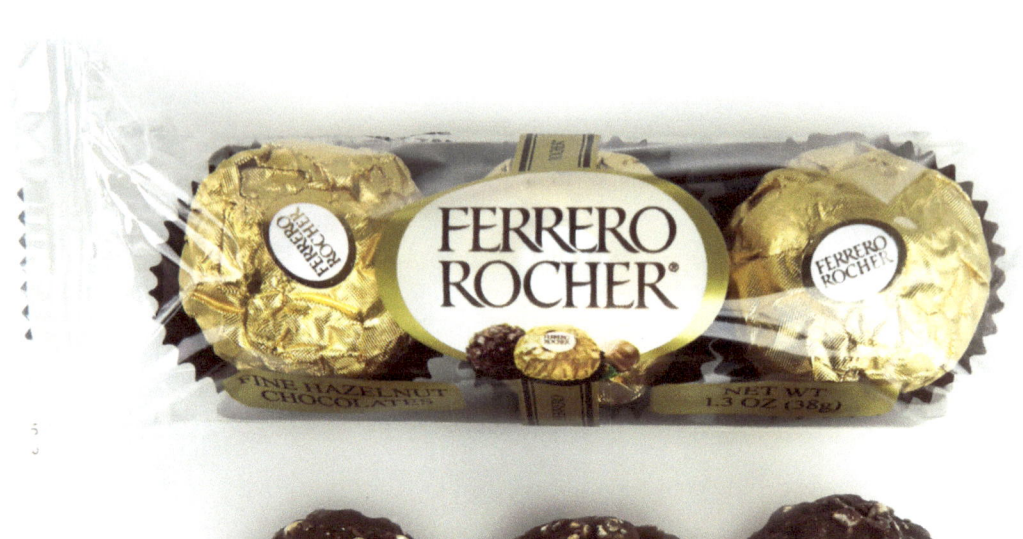
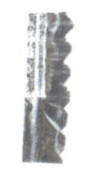
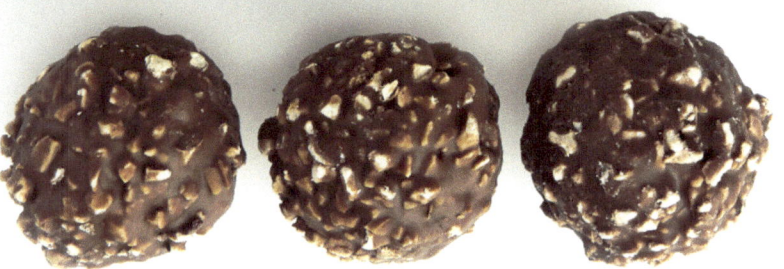

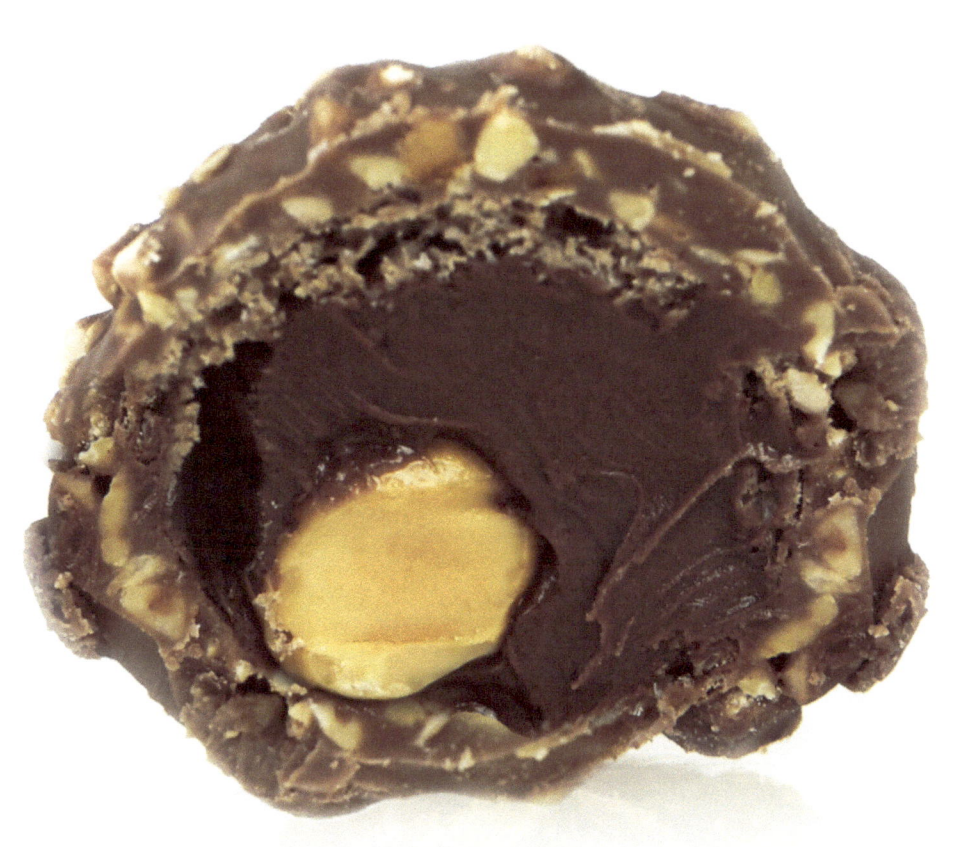

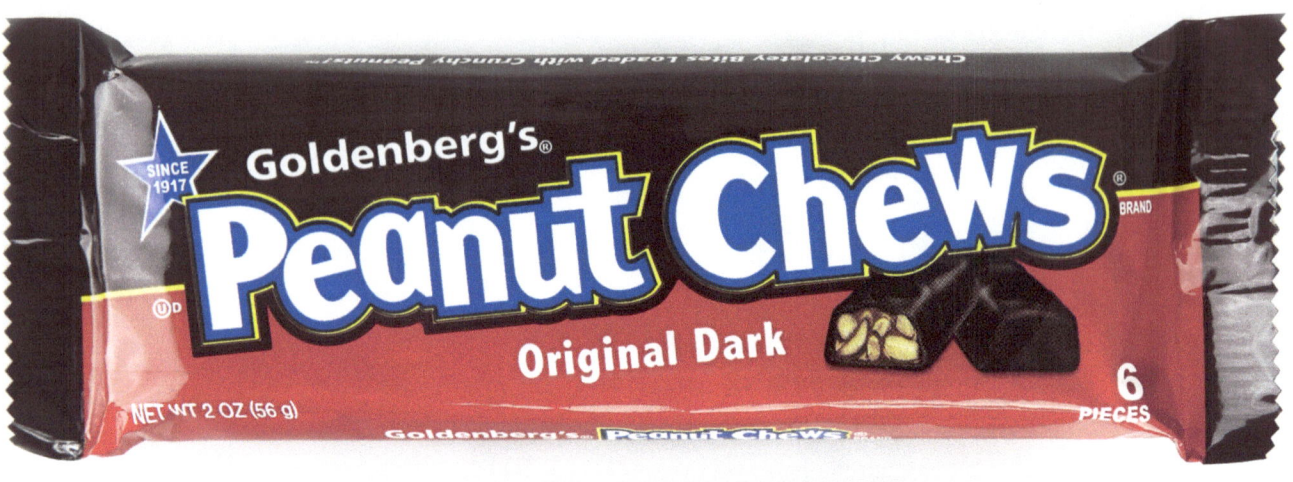

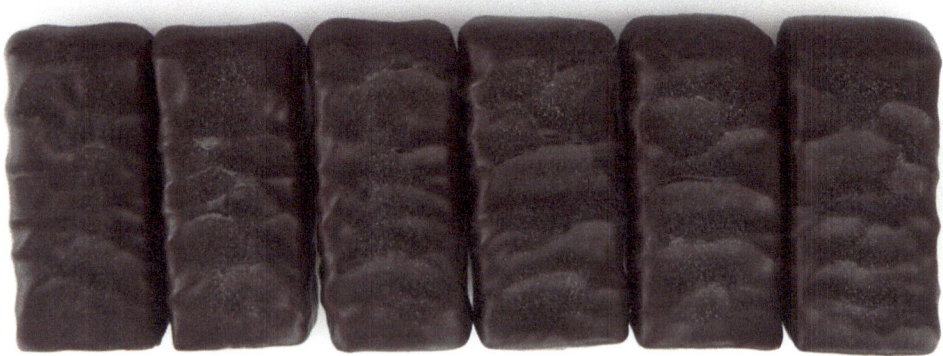

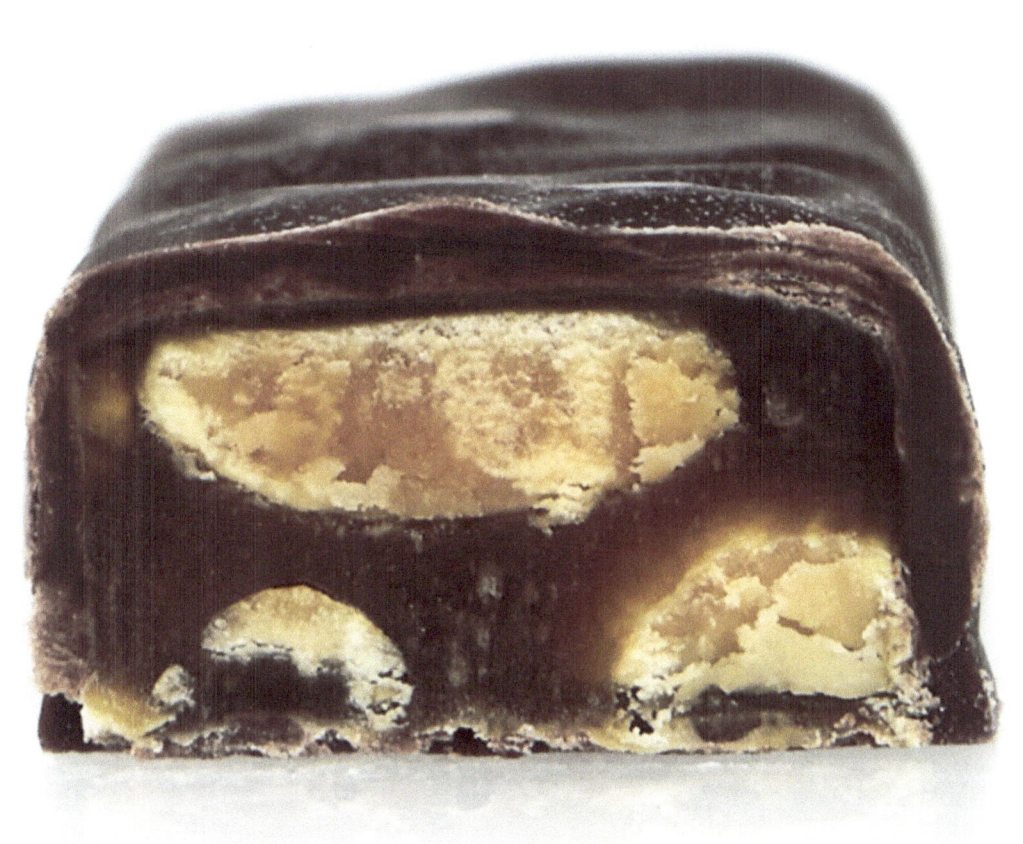

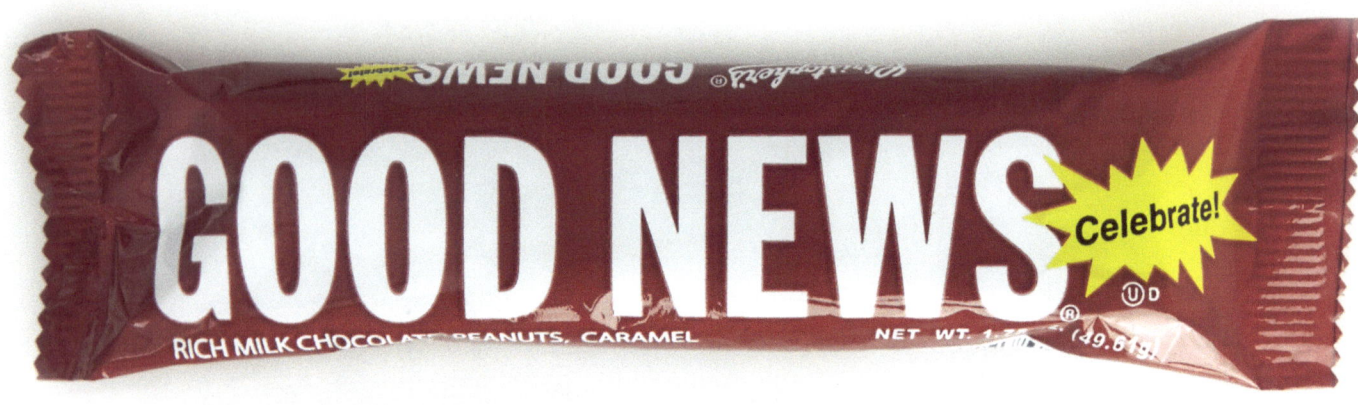

GOOD NEWS Celebrate!

RICH MILK CHOCOLATE PEANUTS, CARAMEL   NET WT. 1.75 (49.61g)

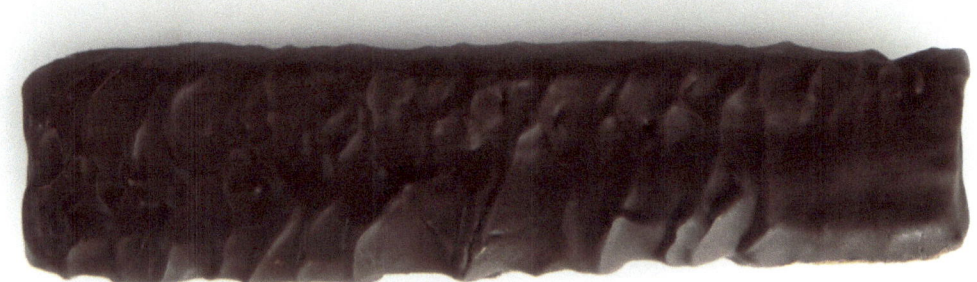

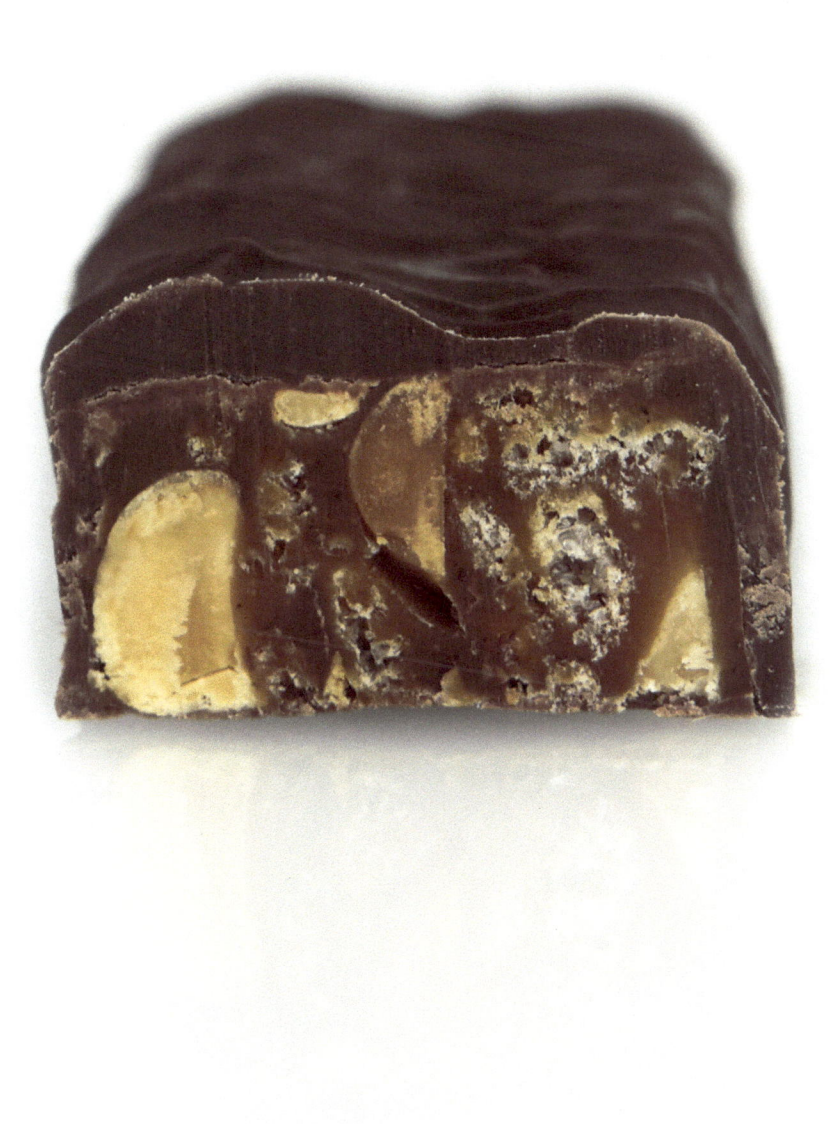

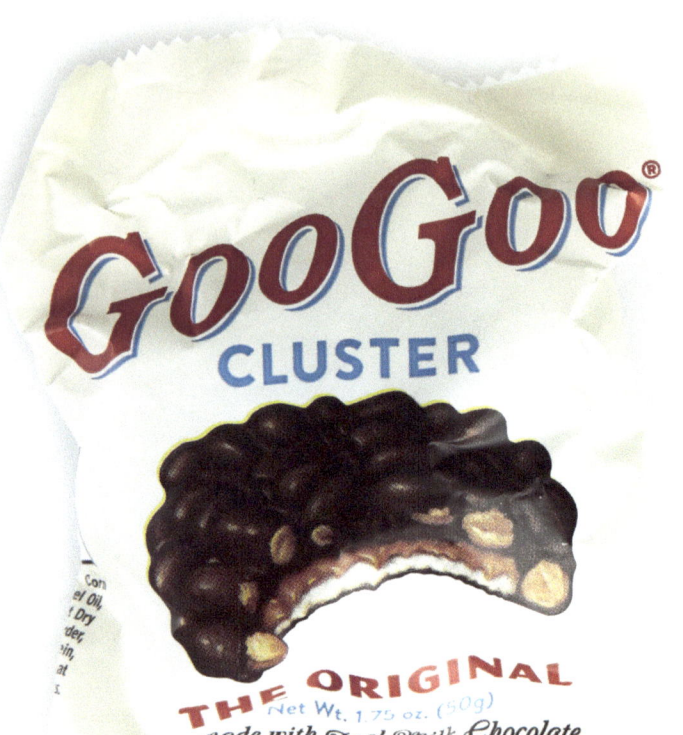

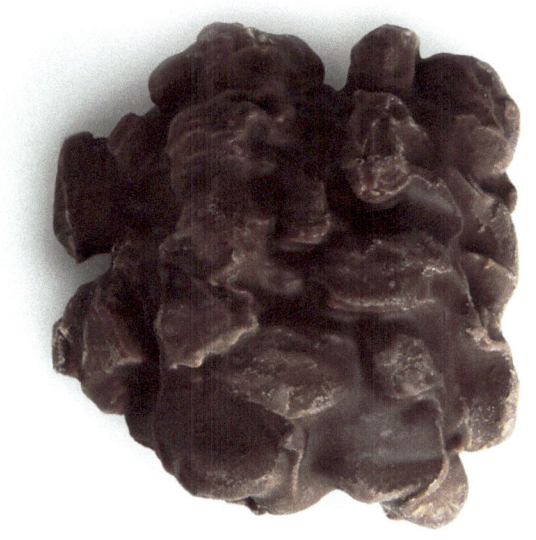

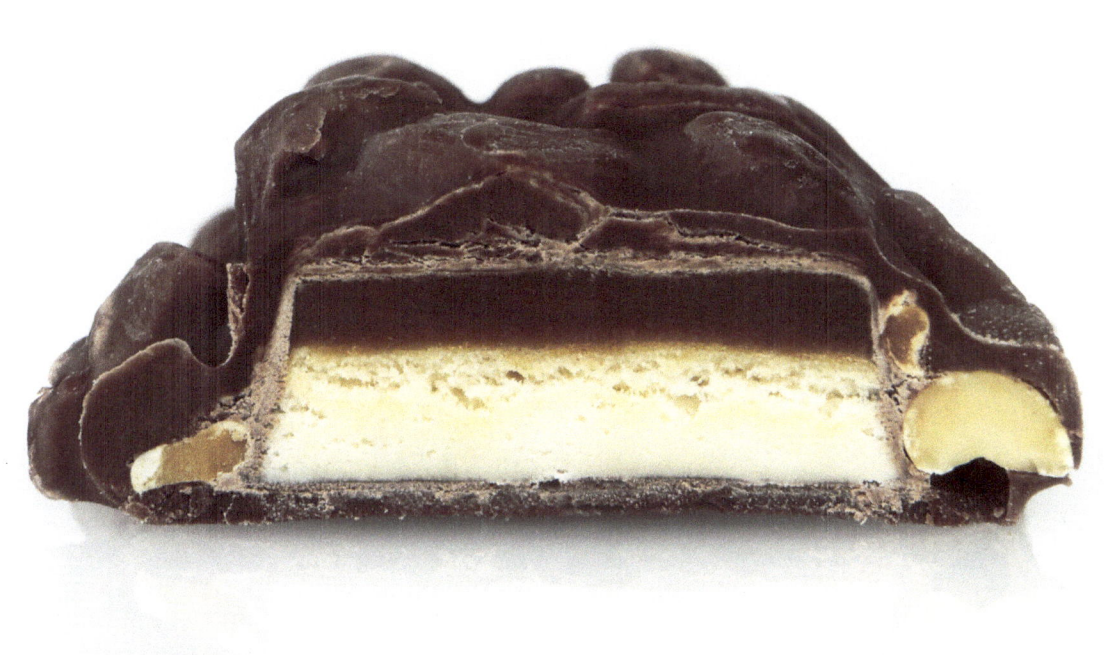

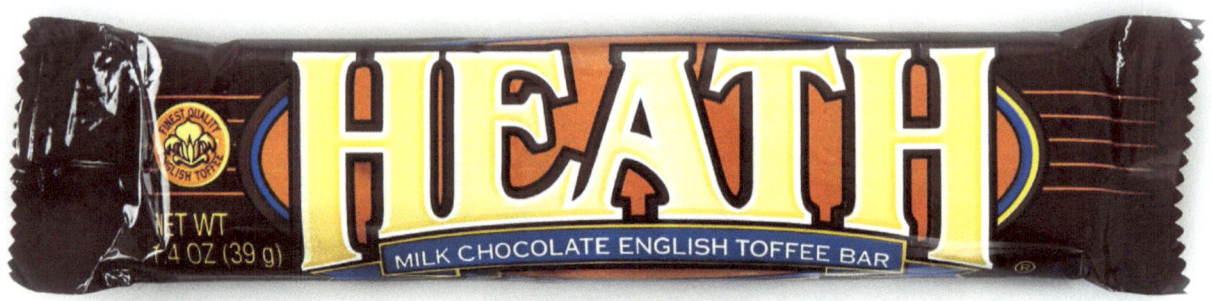

HEATH

MILK CHOCOLATE ENGLISH TOFFEE BAR

NET WT 1.4 OZ (39 g)

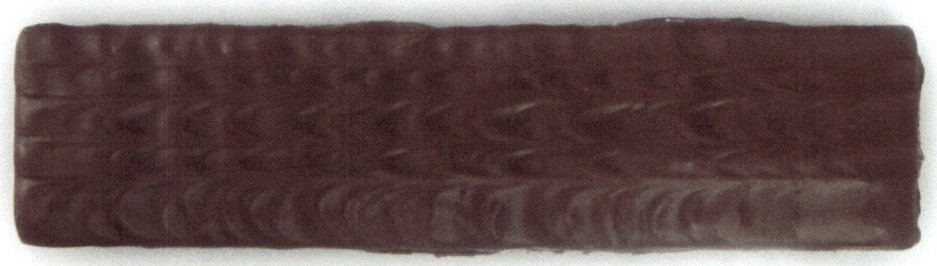

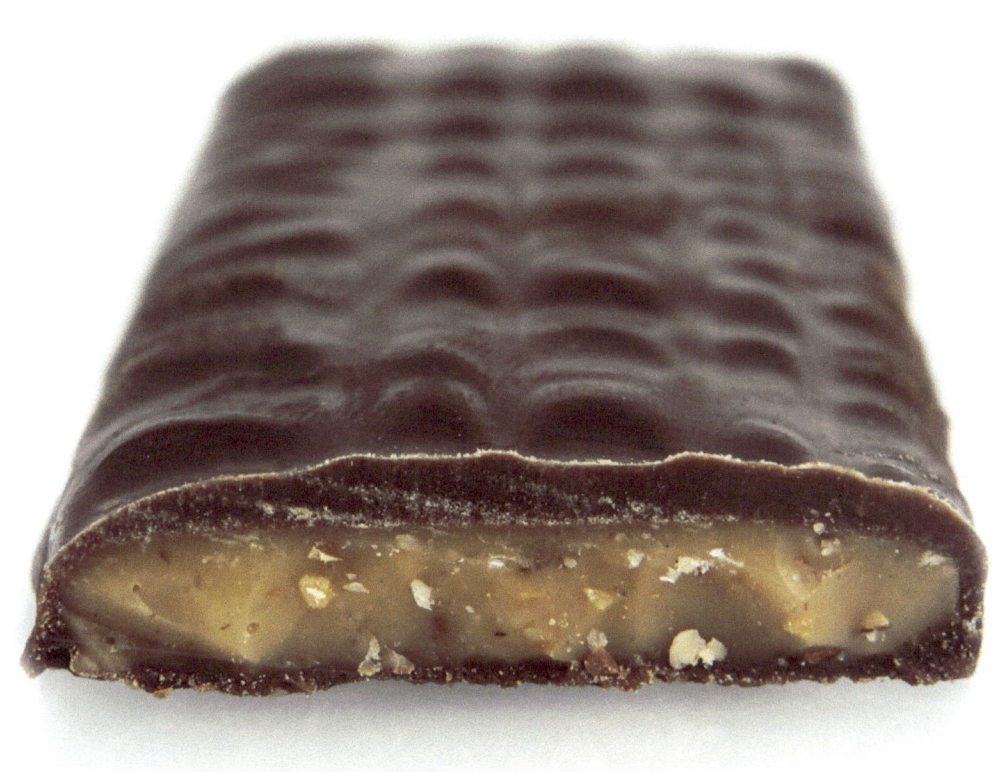

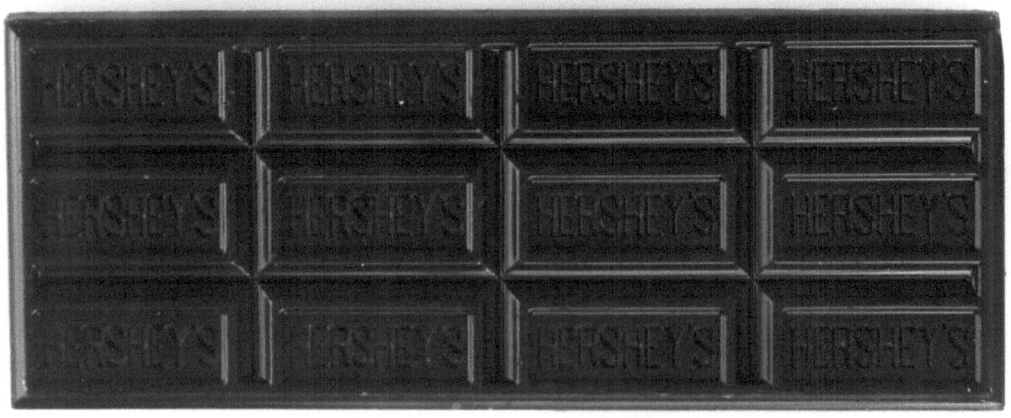

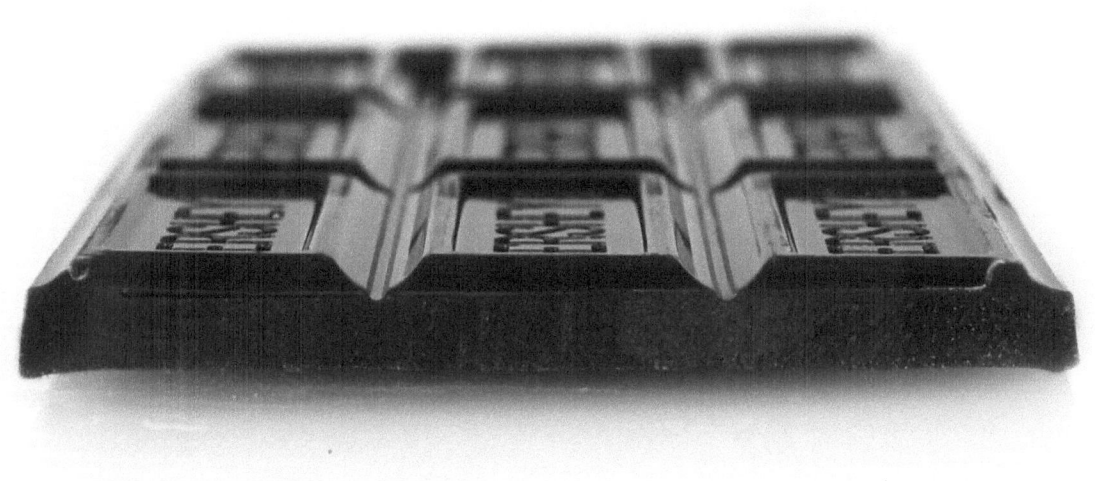

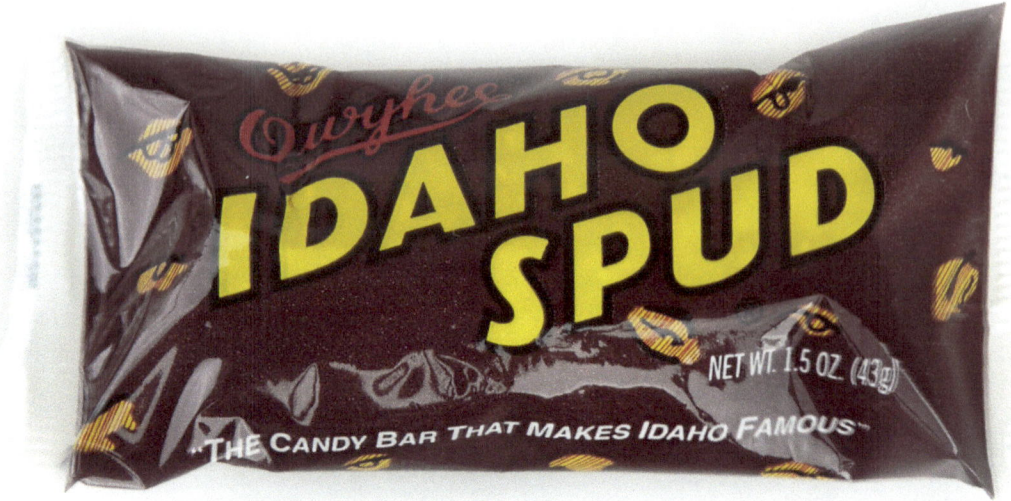

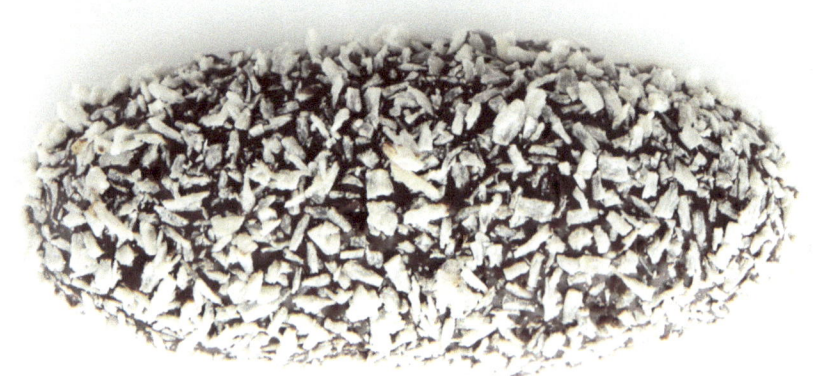

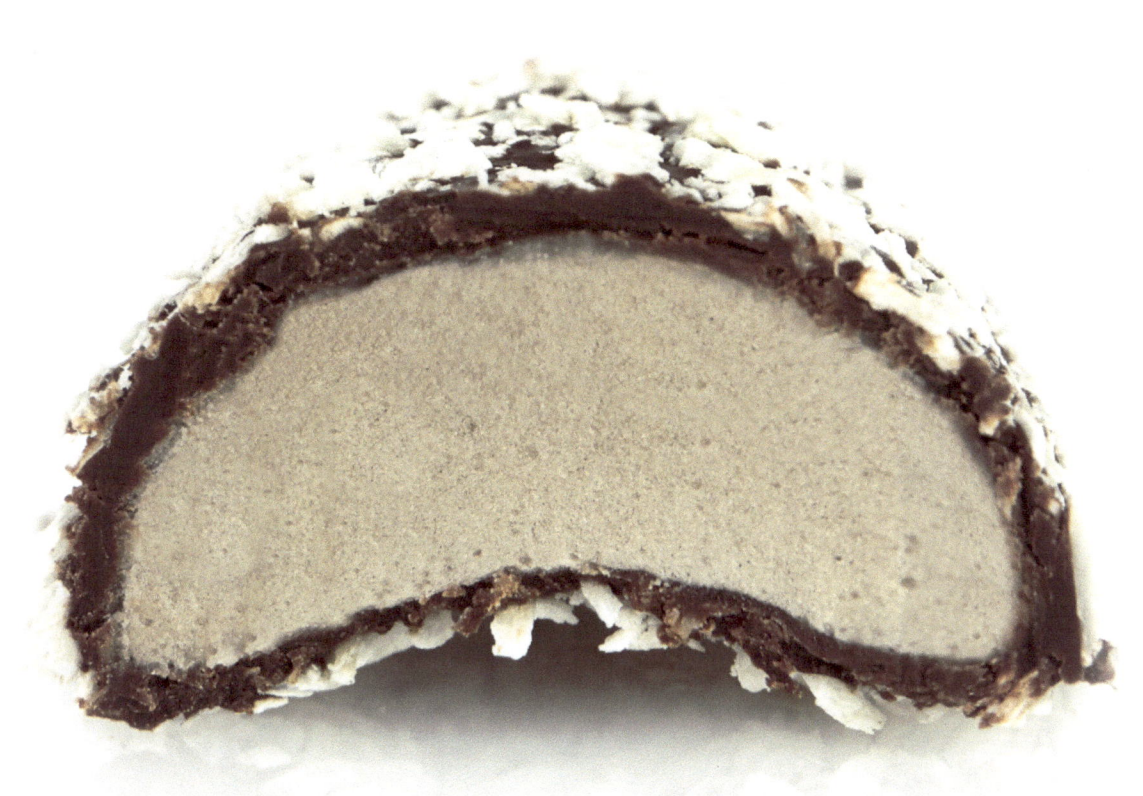

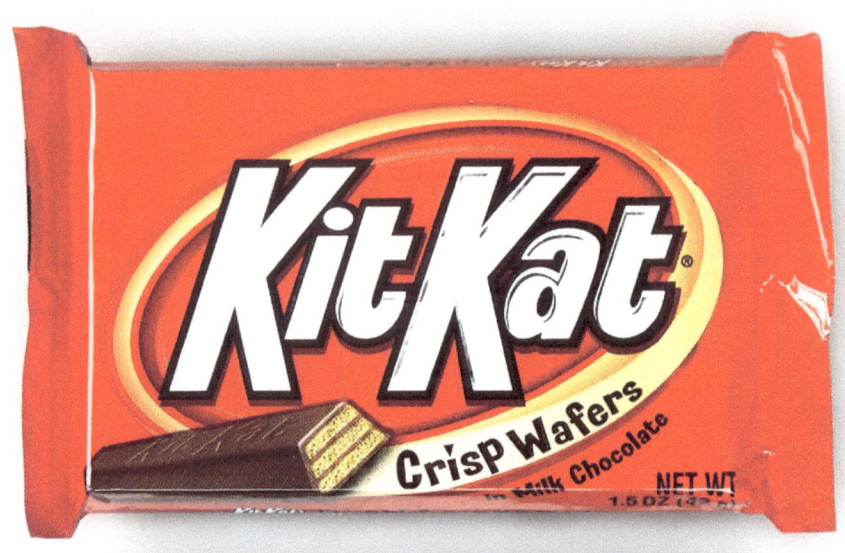

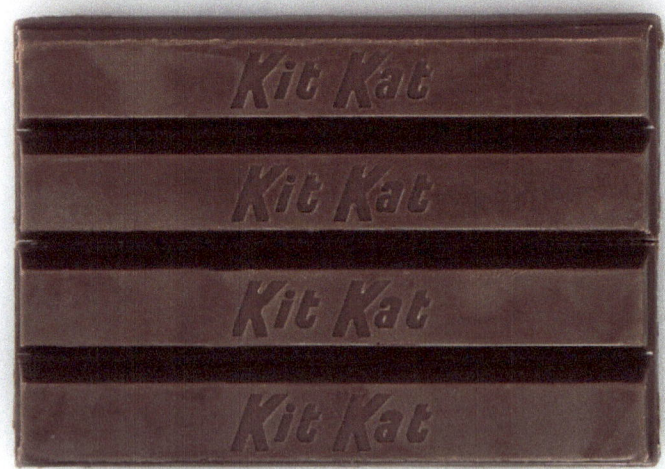

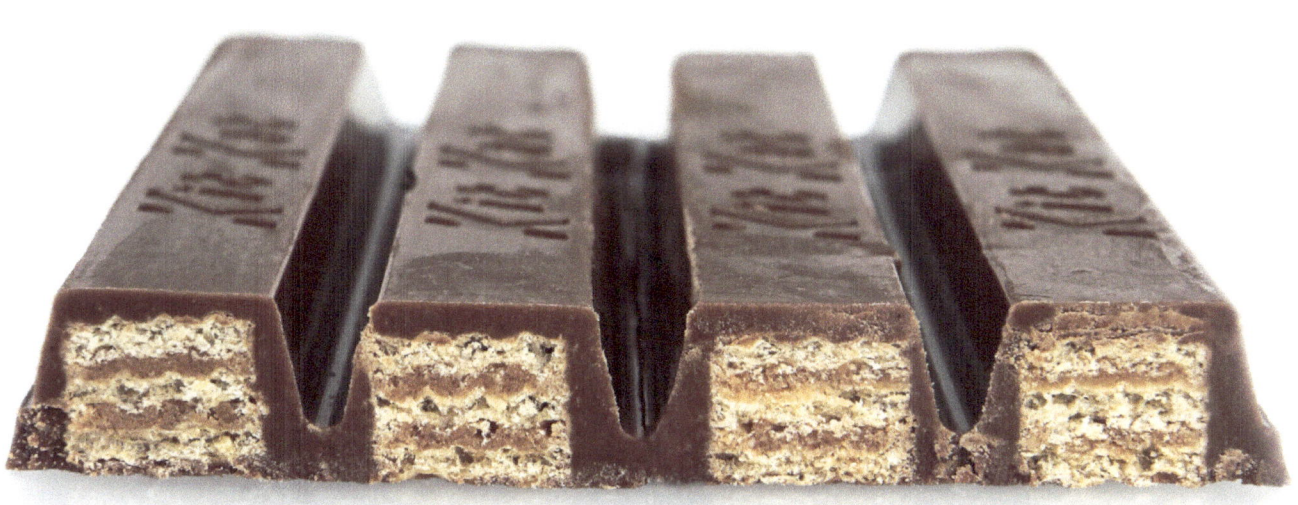

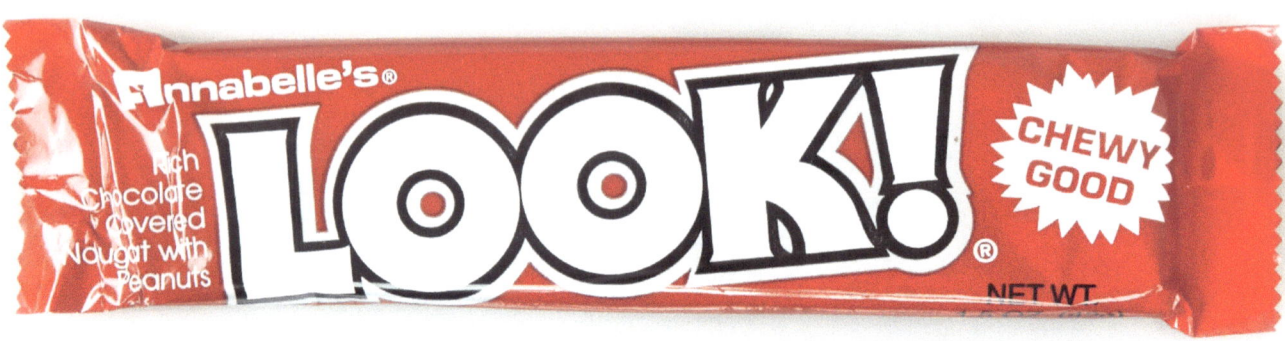

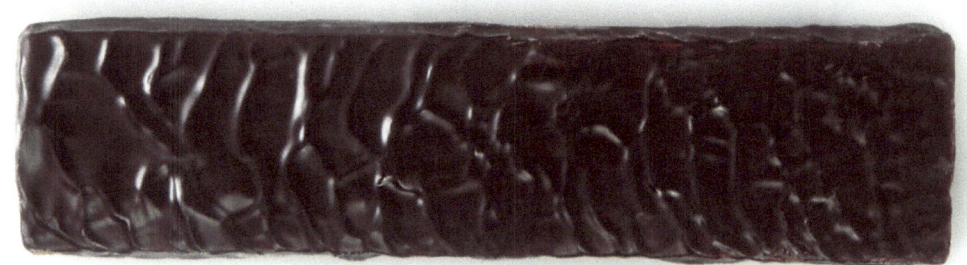

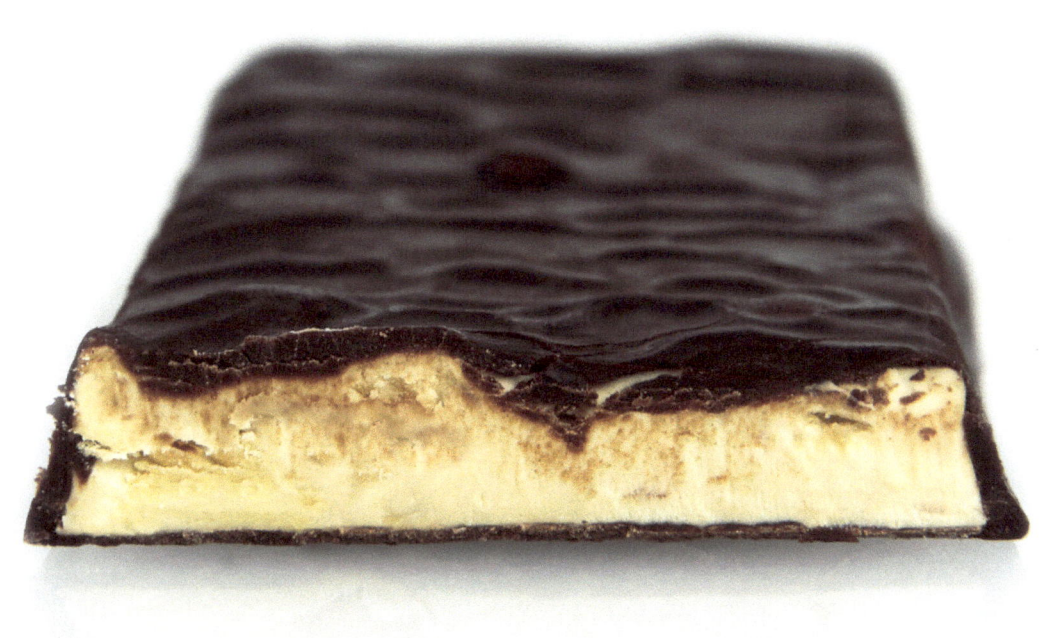

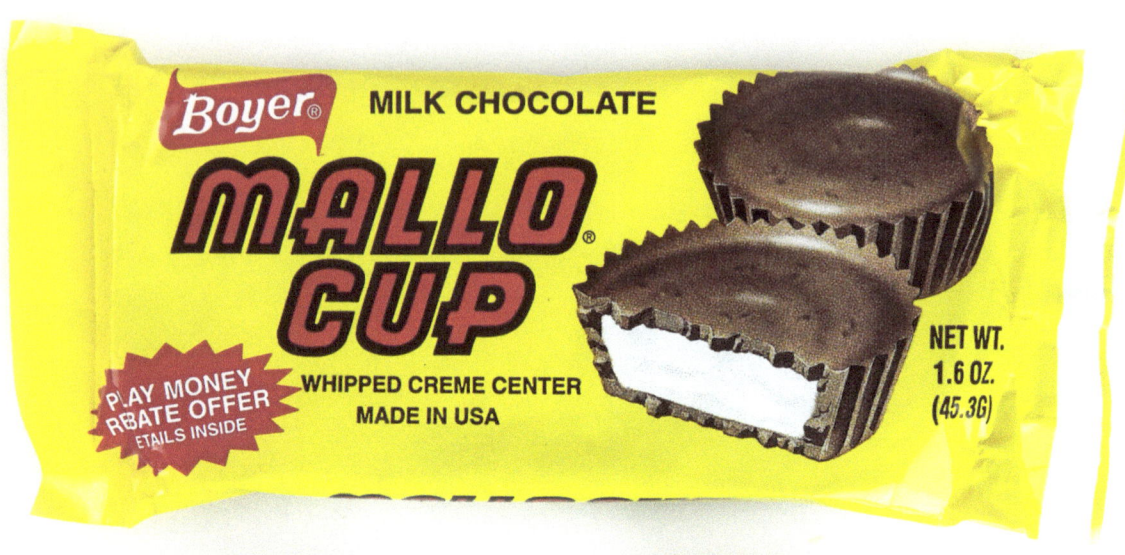

Boyer®

MILK CHOCOLATE

MALLO CUP®

PLAY MONEY RBATE OFFER ETAILS INSIDE

WHIPPED CREME CENTER
MADE IN USA

NET WT.
1.6 OZ.
(45.3G)

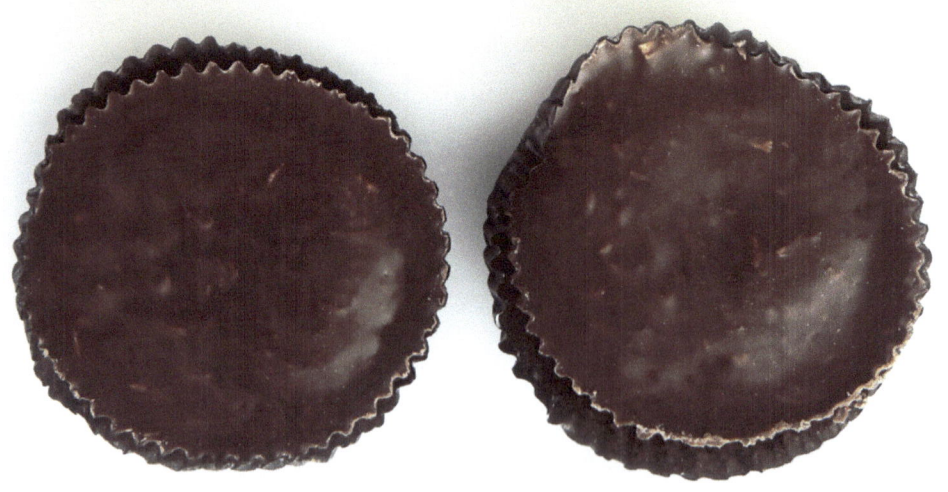

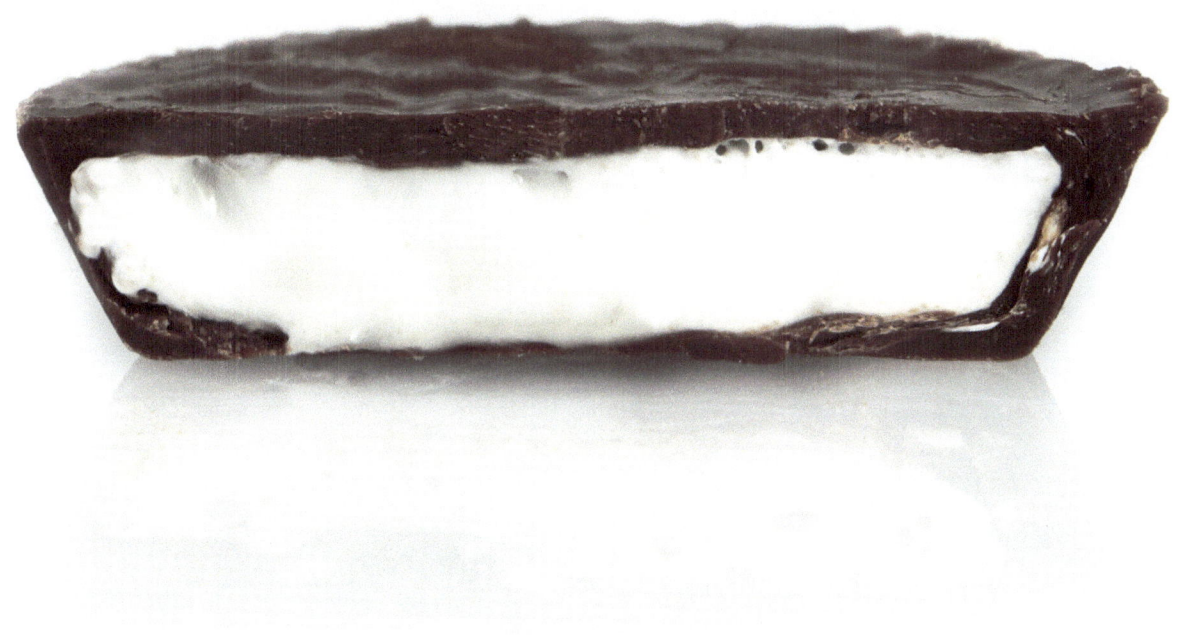

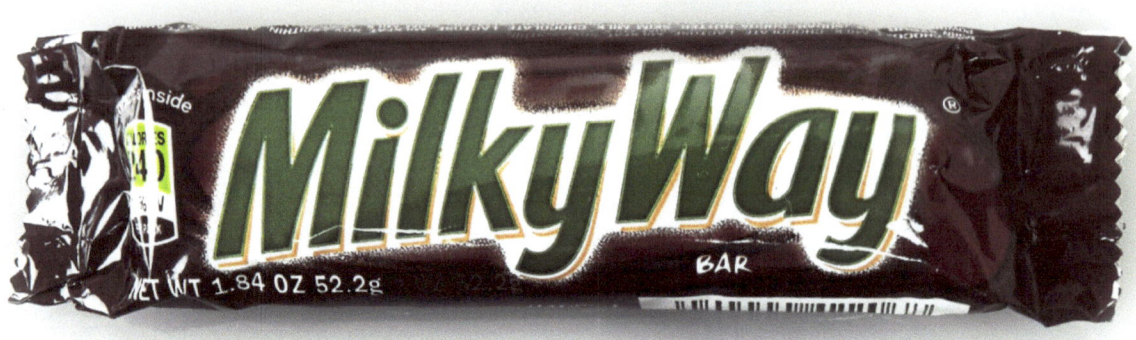

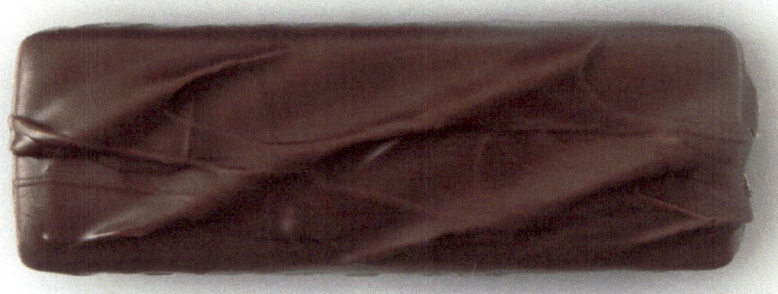

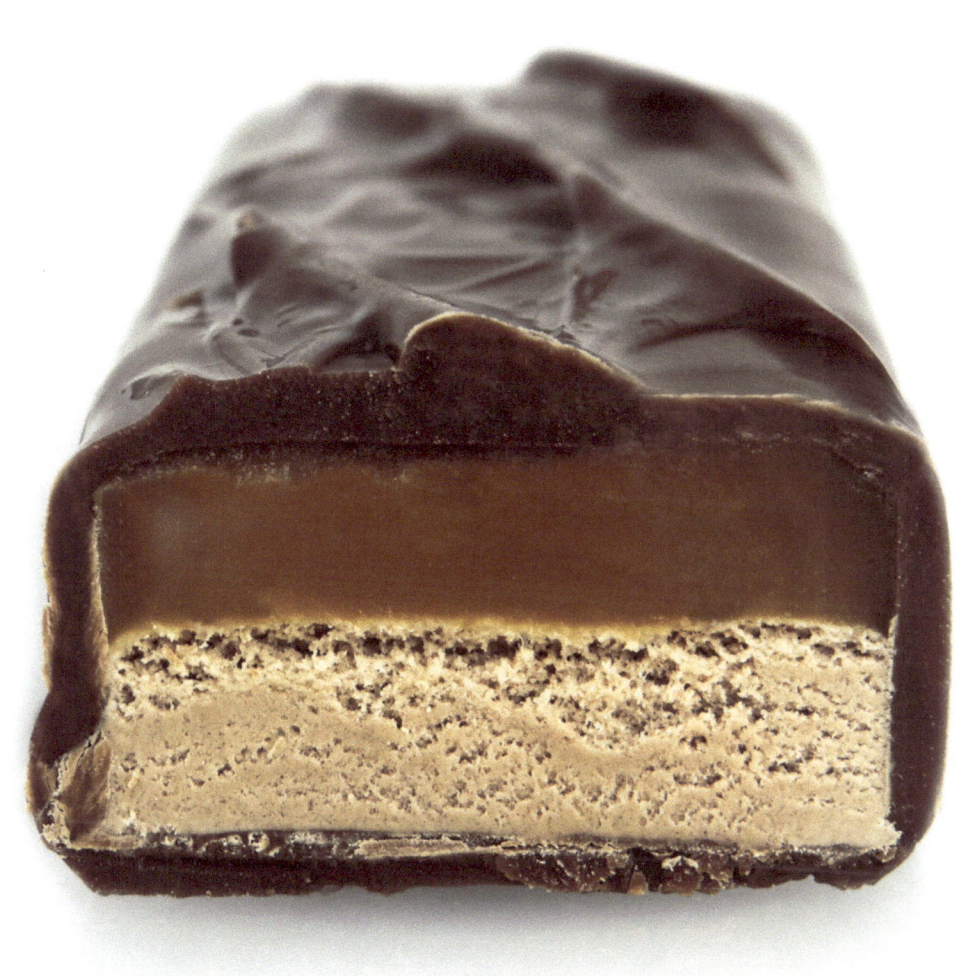

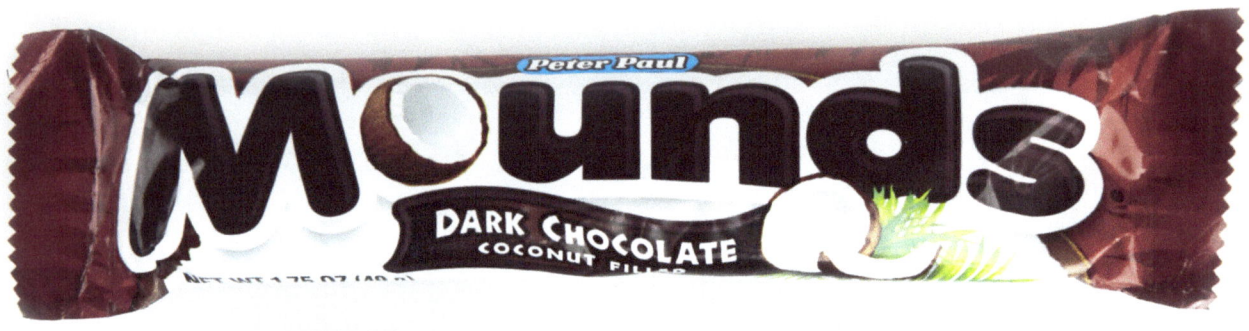
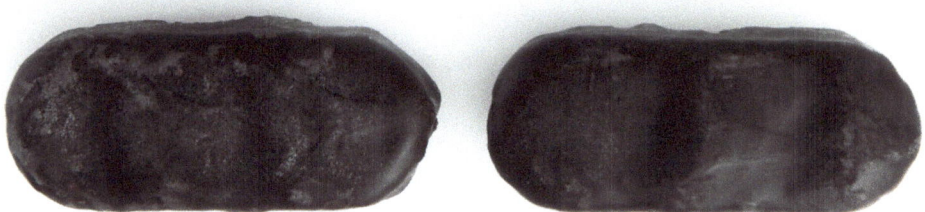

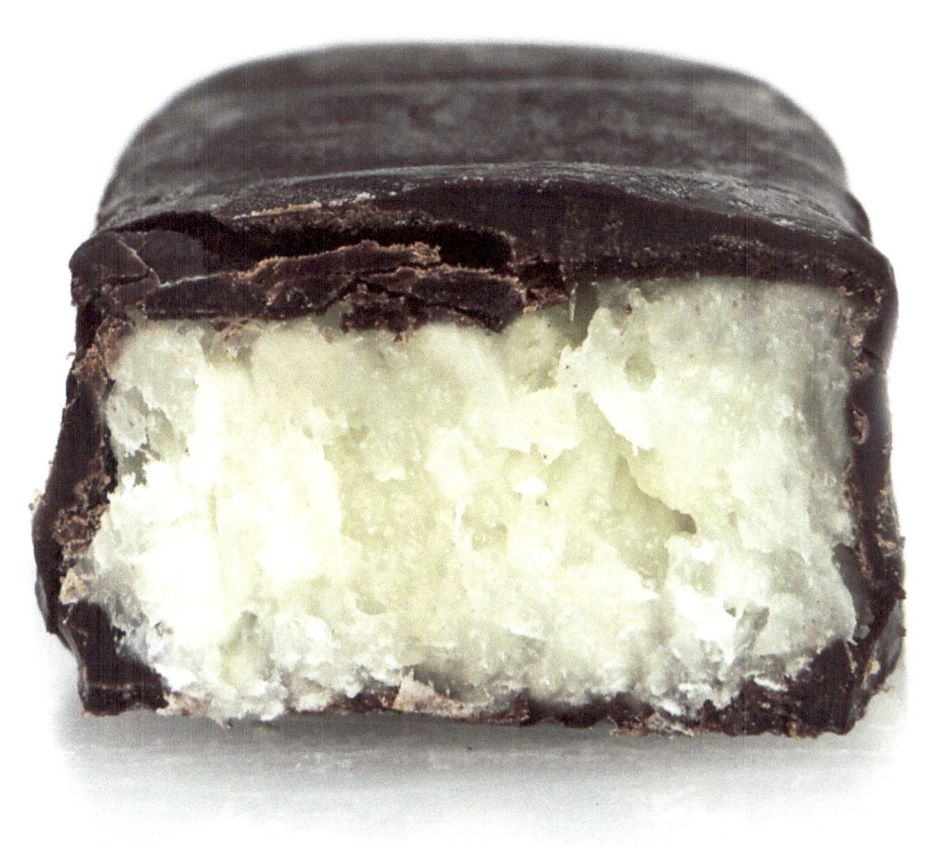

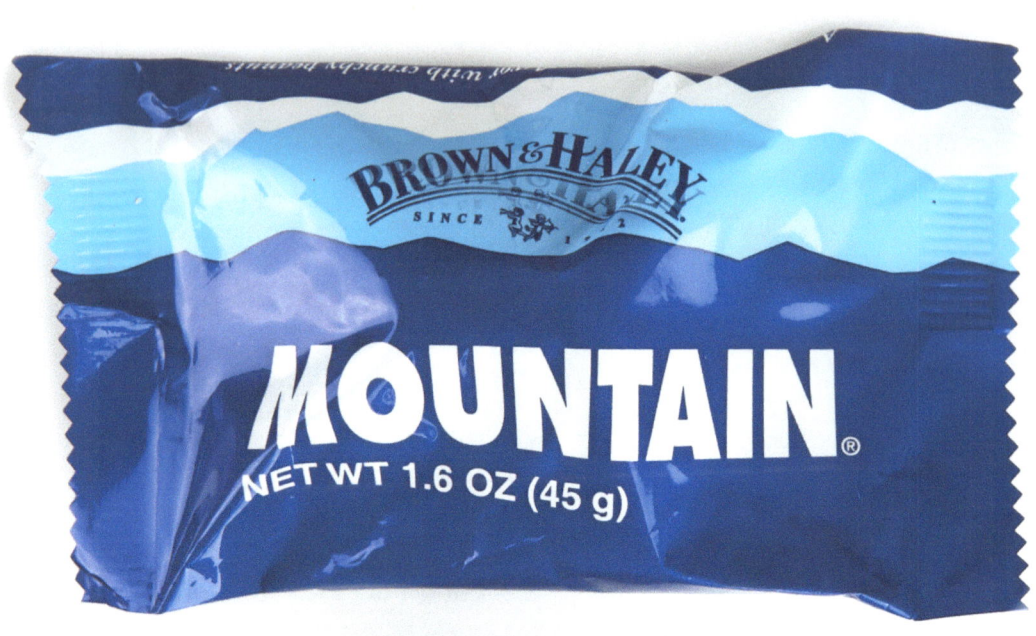

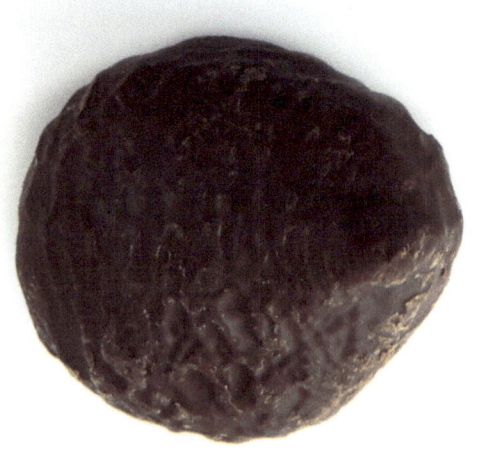

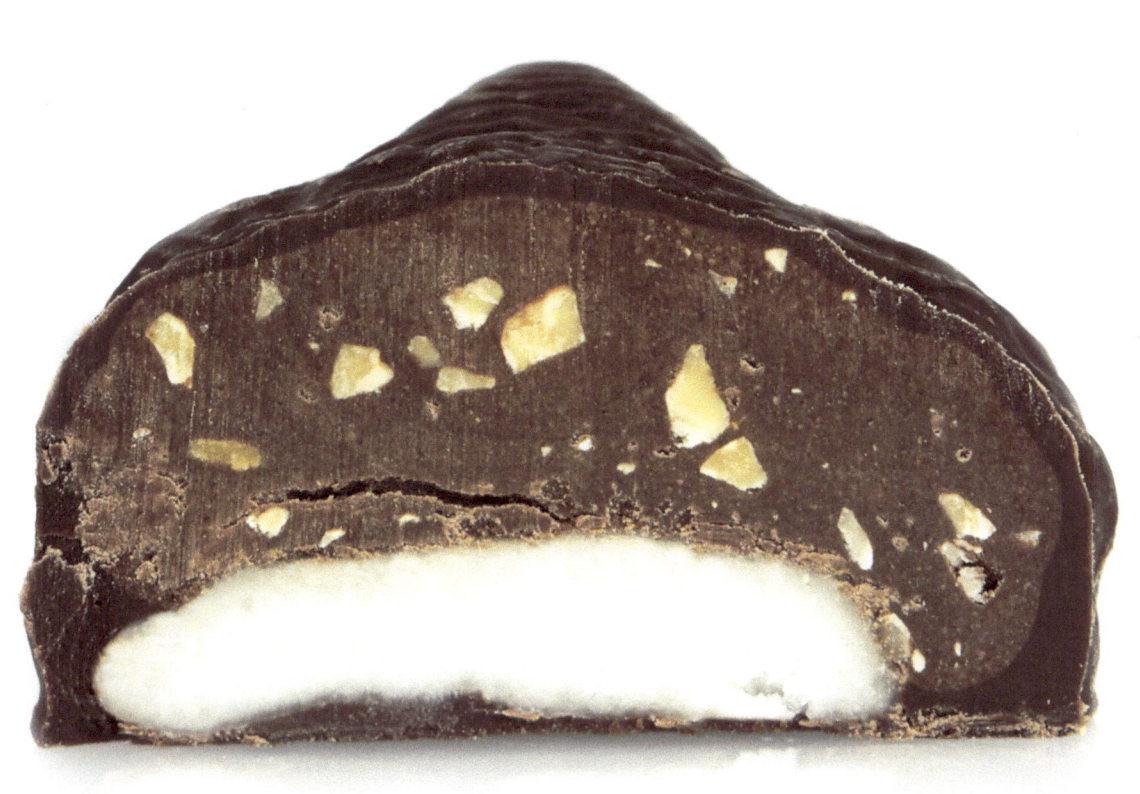

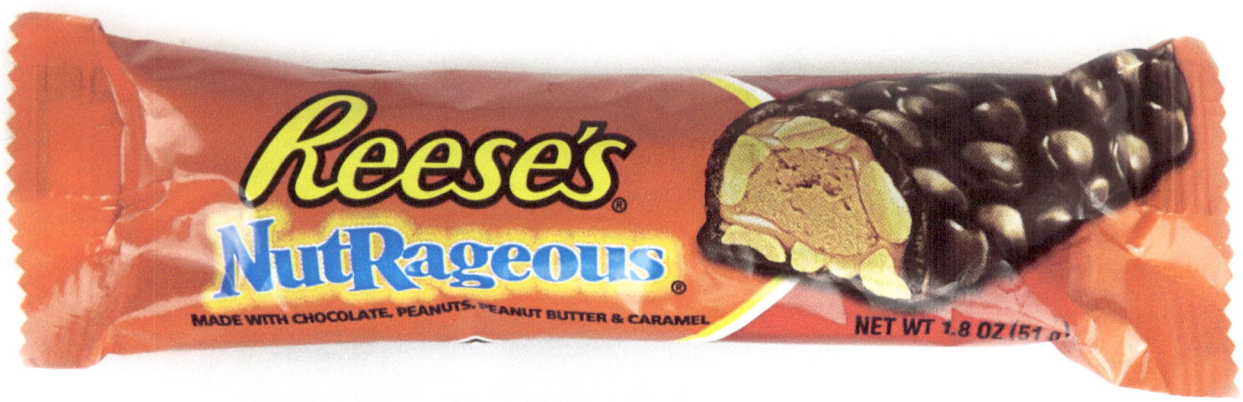

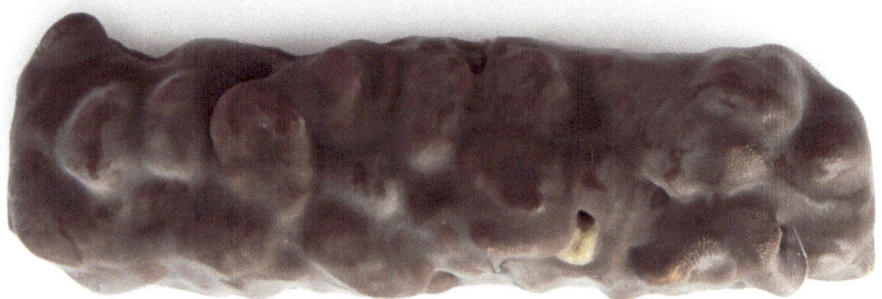

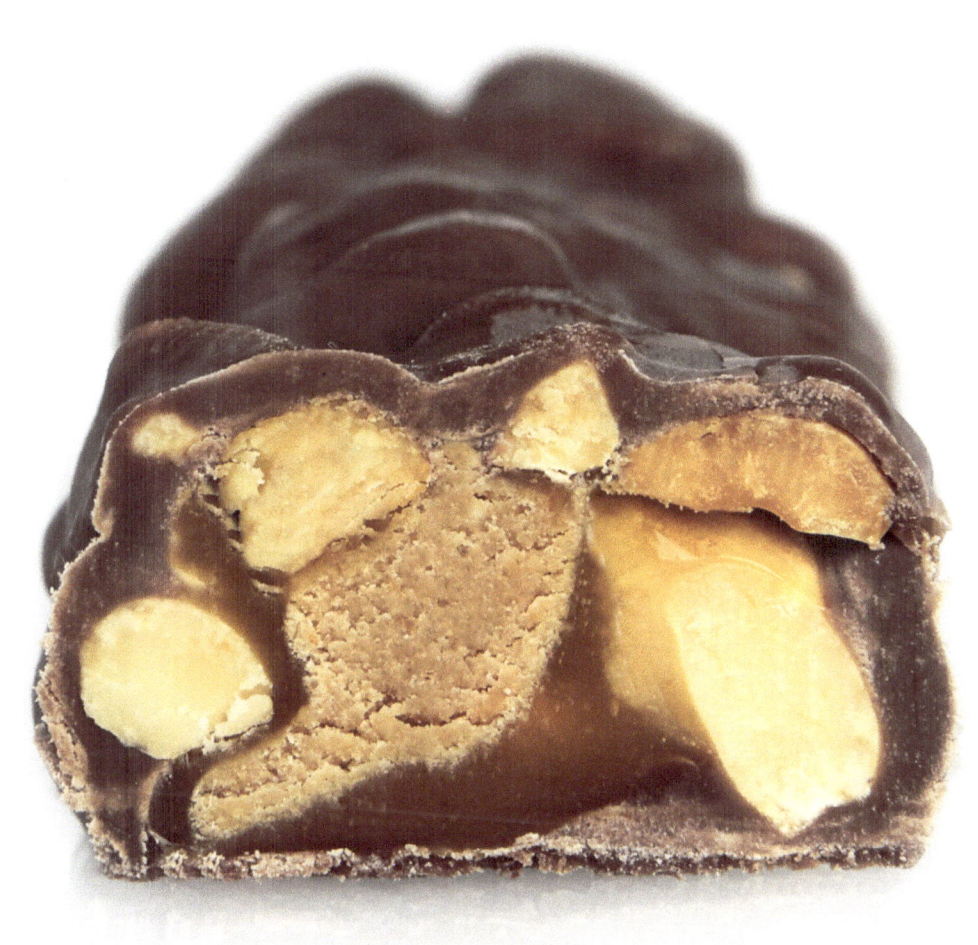

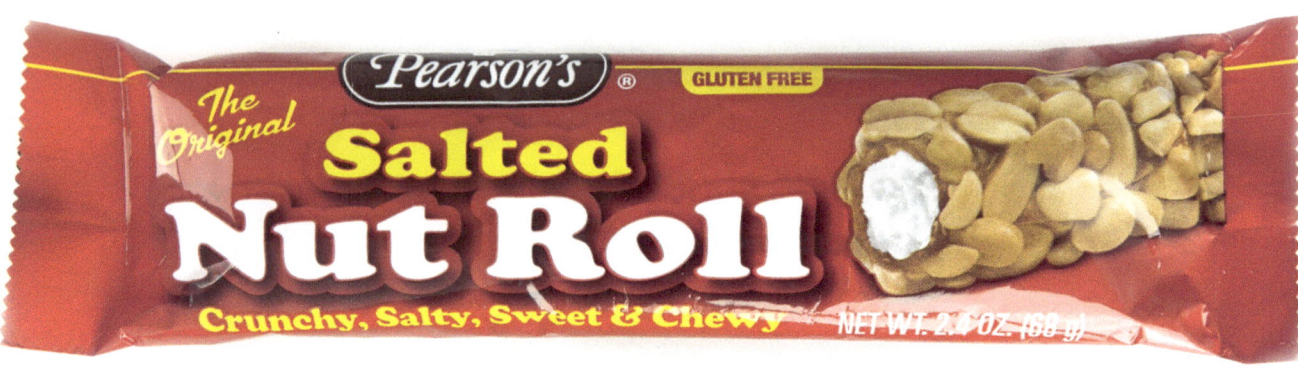

Pearson's®
The Original
Salted
Nut Roll
Crunchy, Salty, Sweet & Chewy
GLUTEN FREE
NET WT. 2.4 OZ. (68 g)

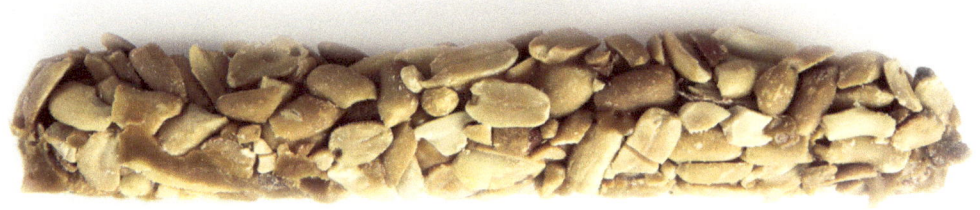

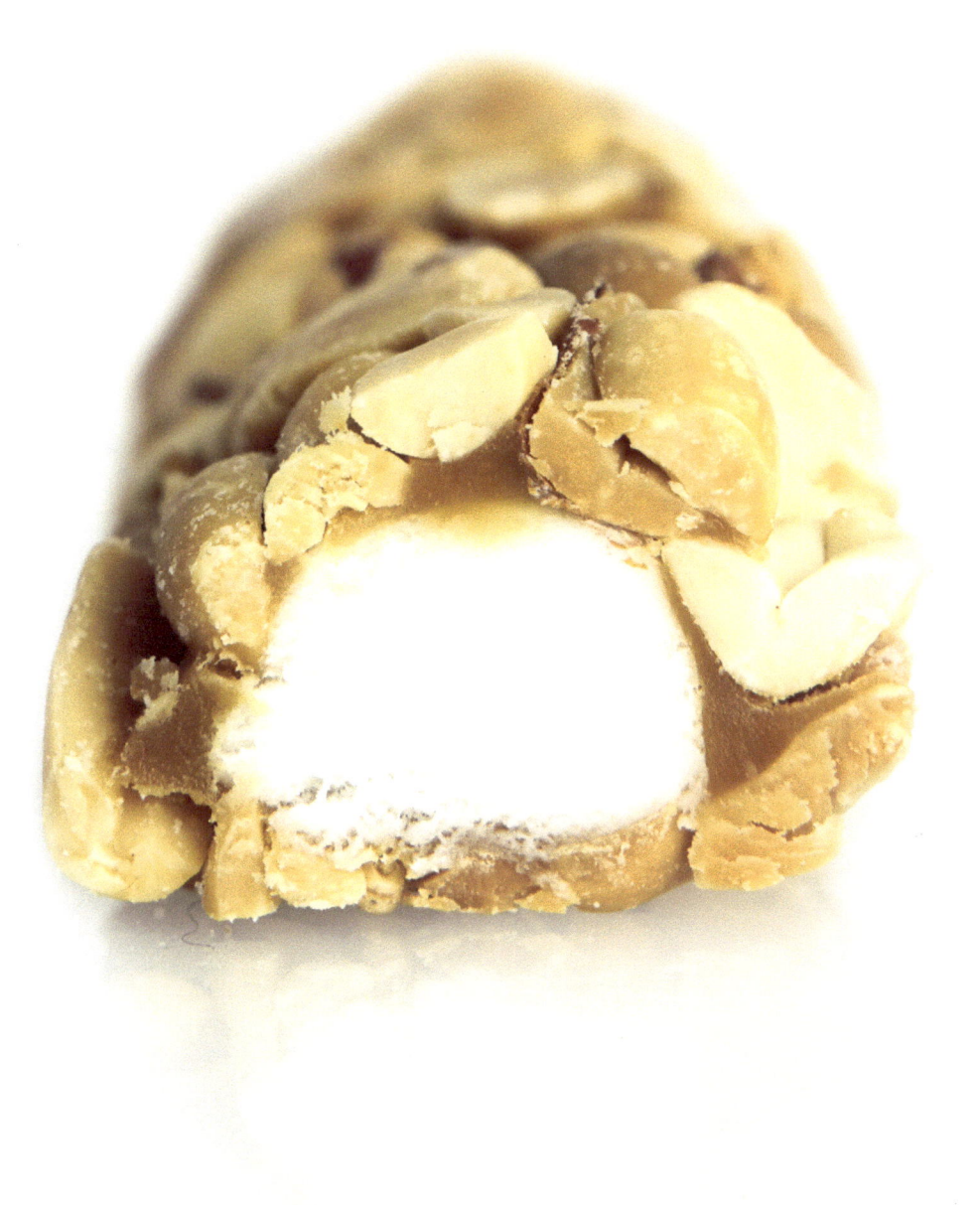

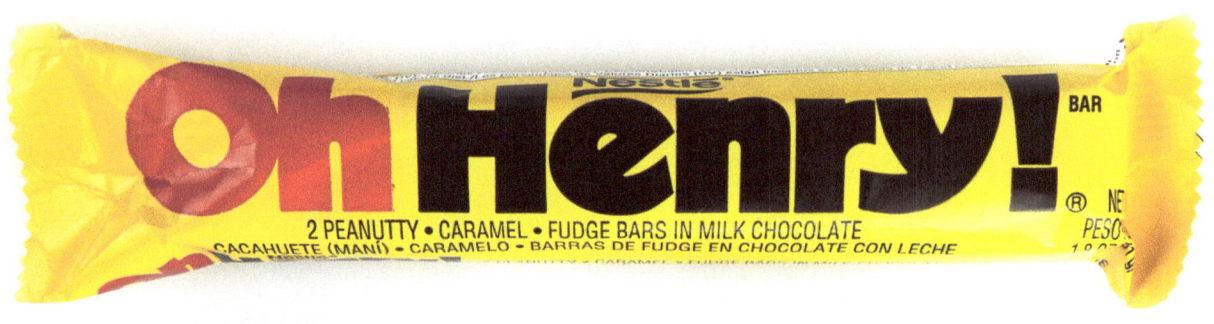

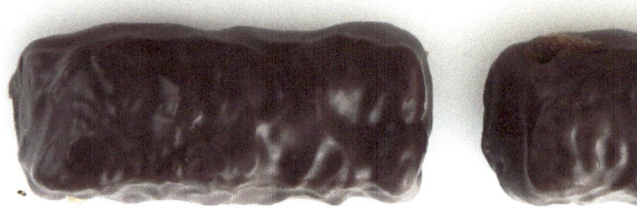 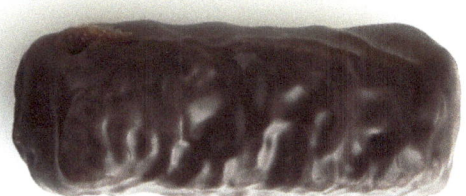

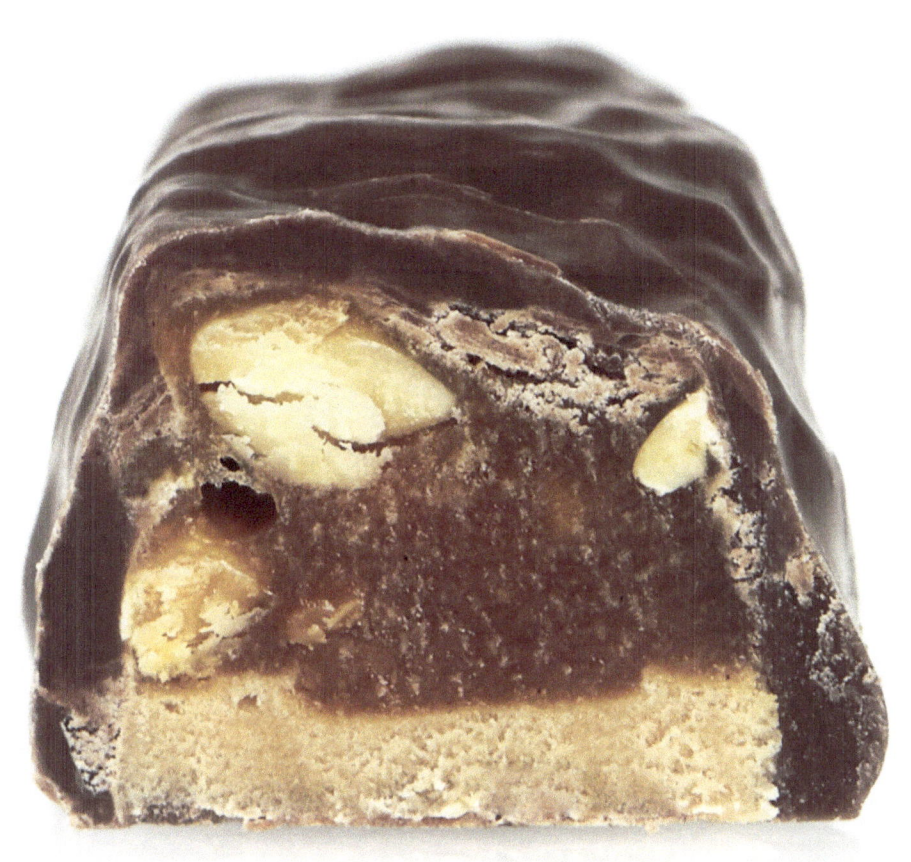

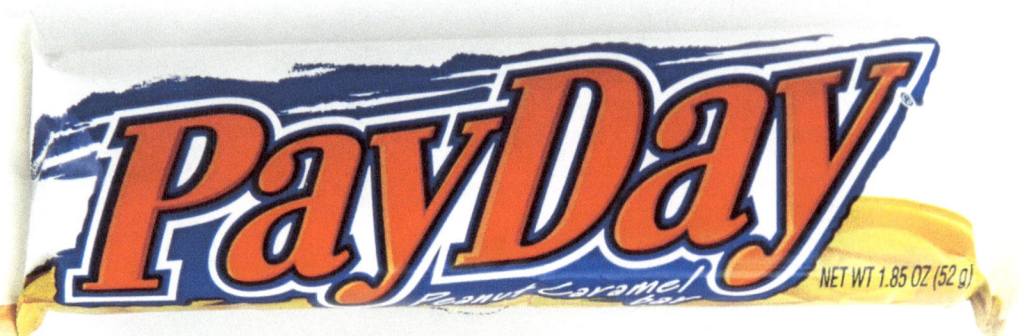

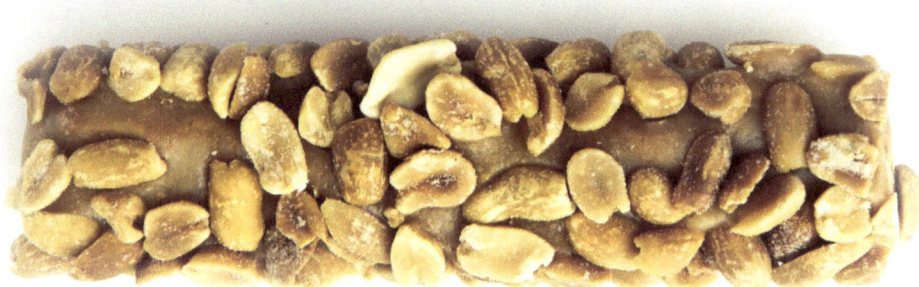

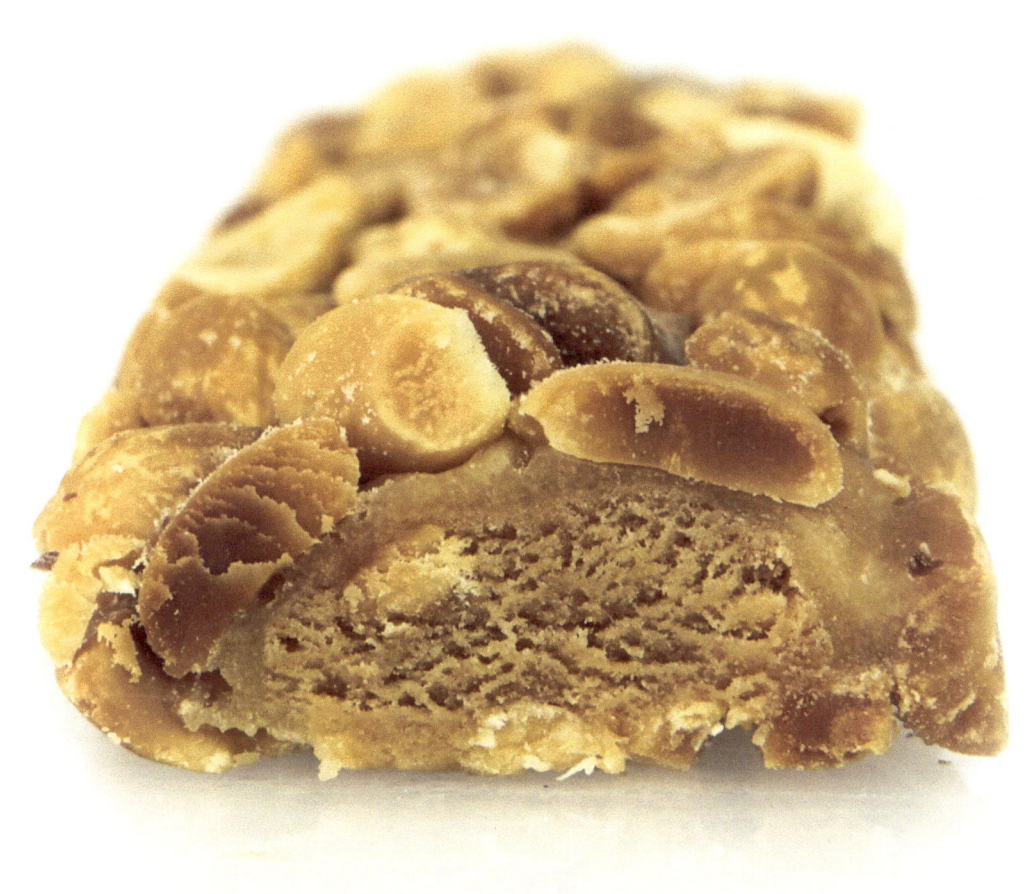

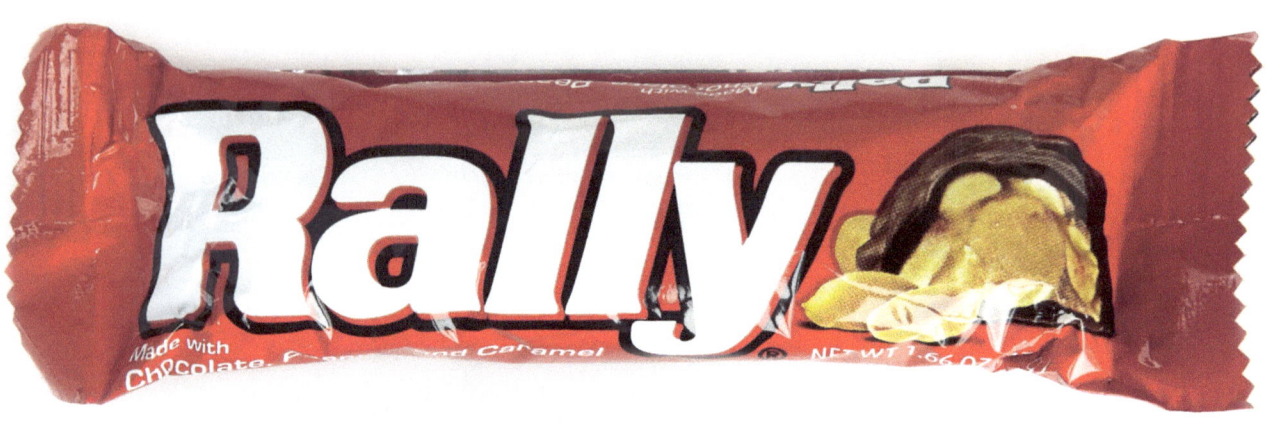

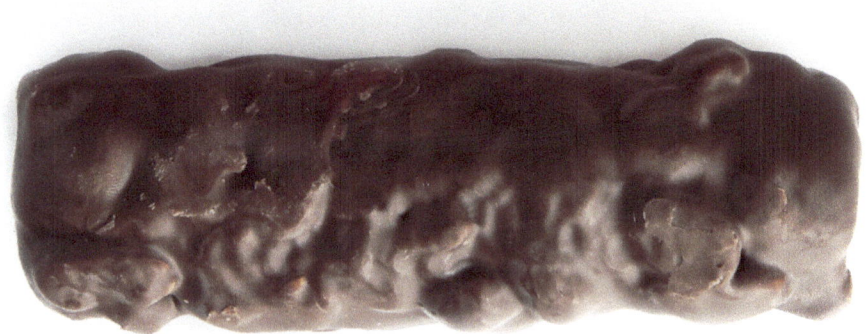

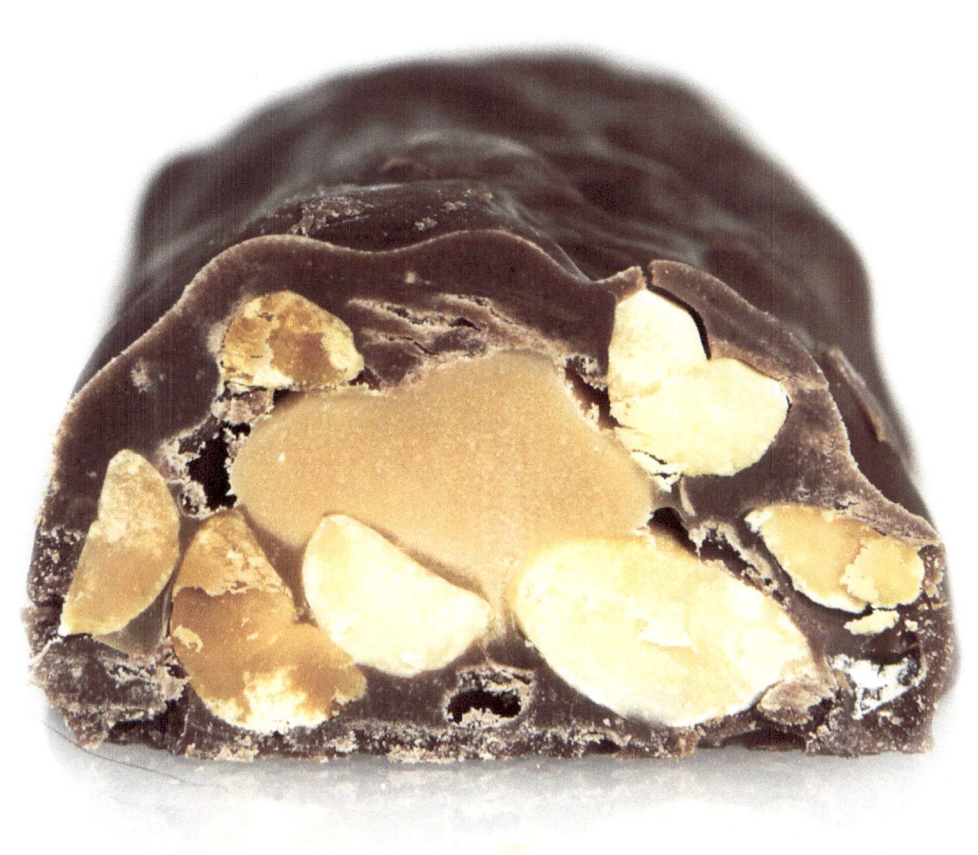

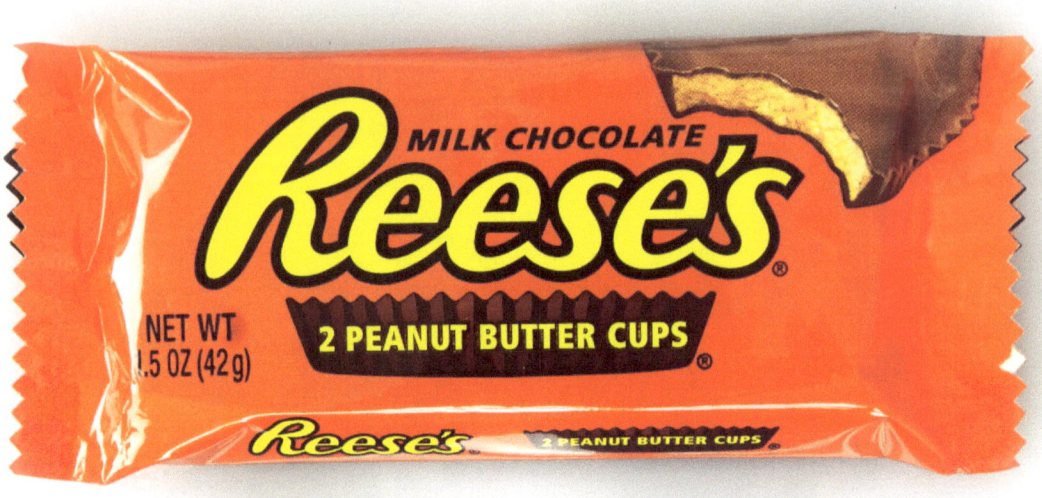

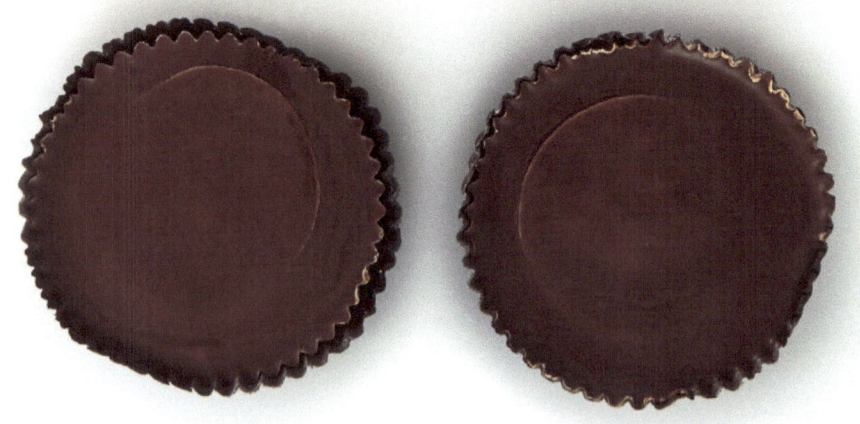

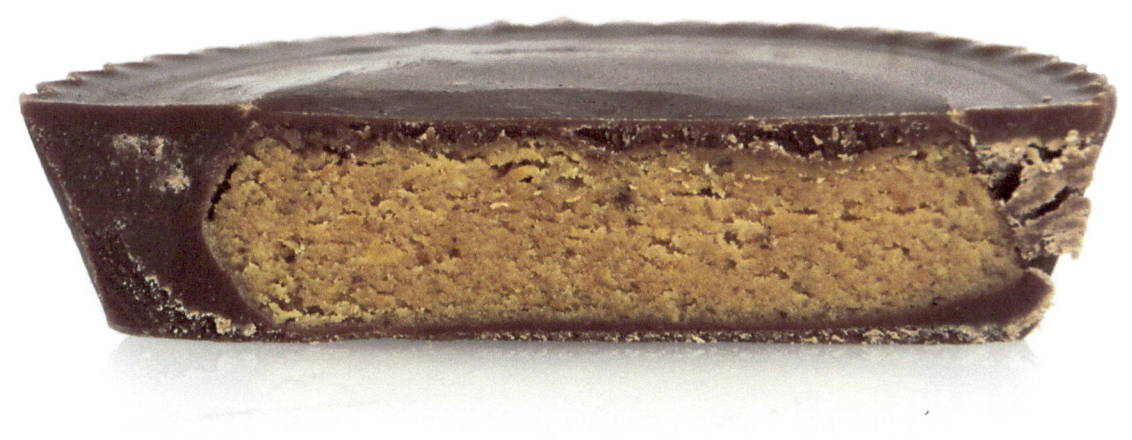

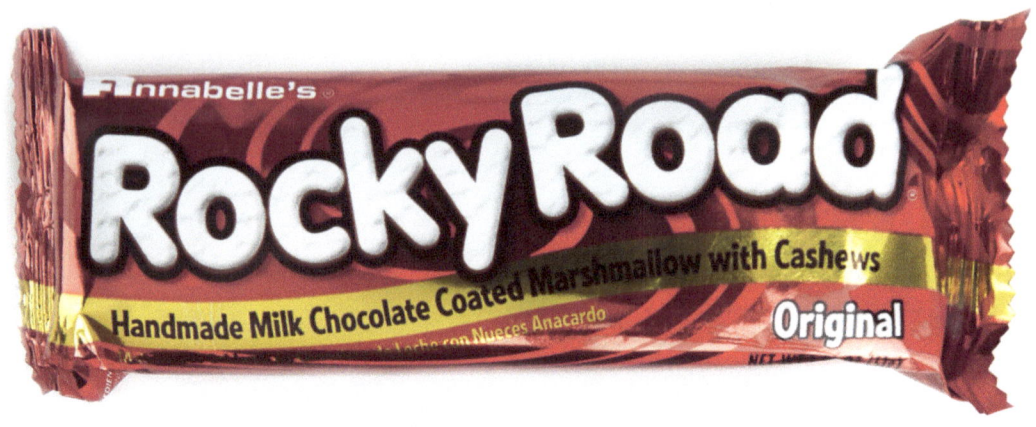

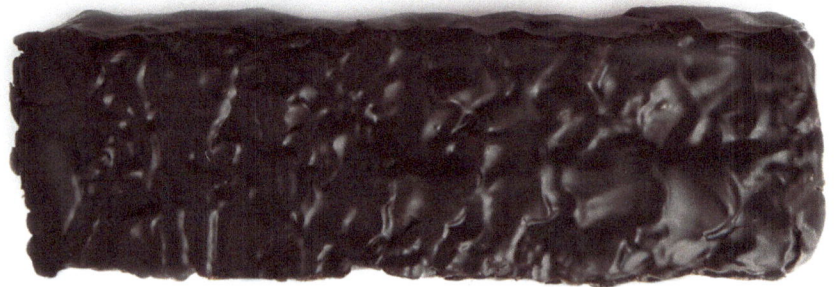

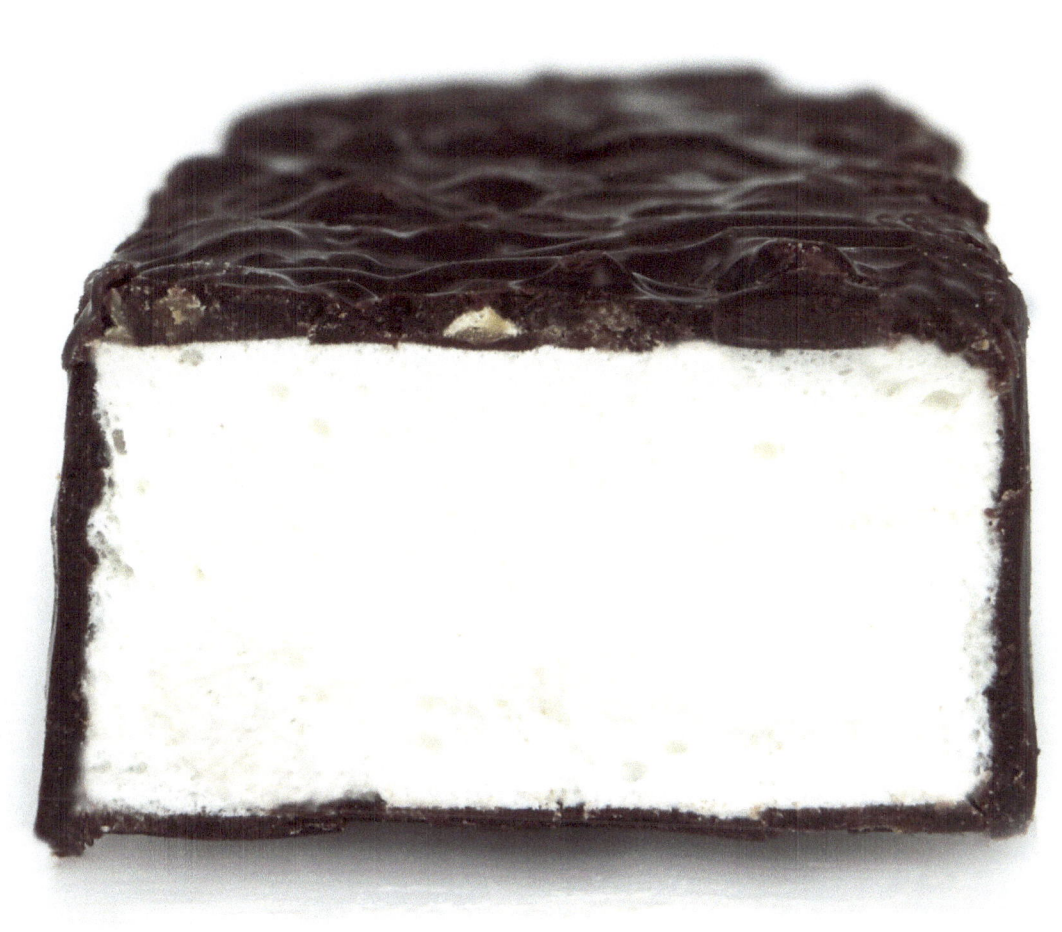

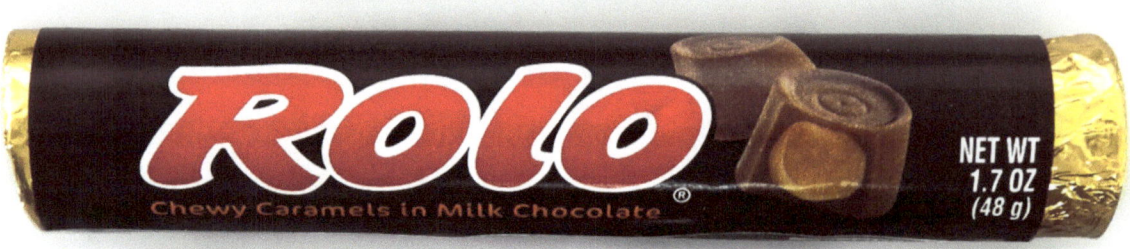

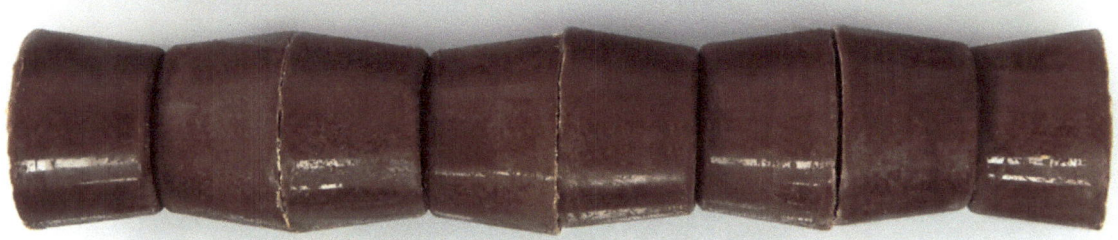

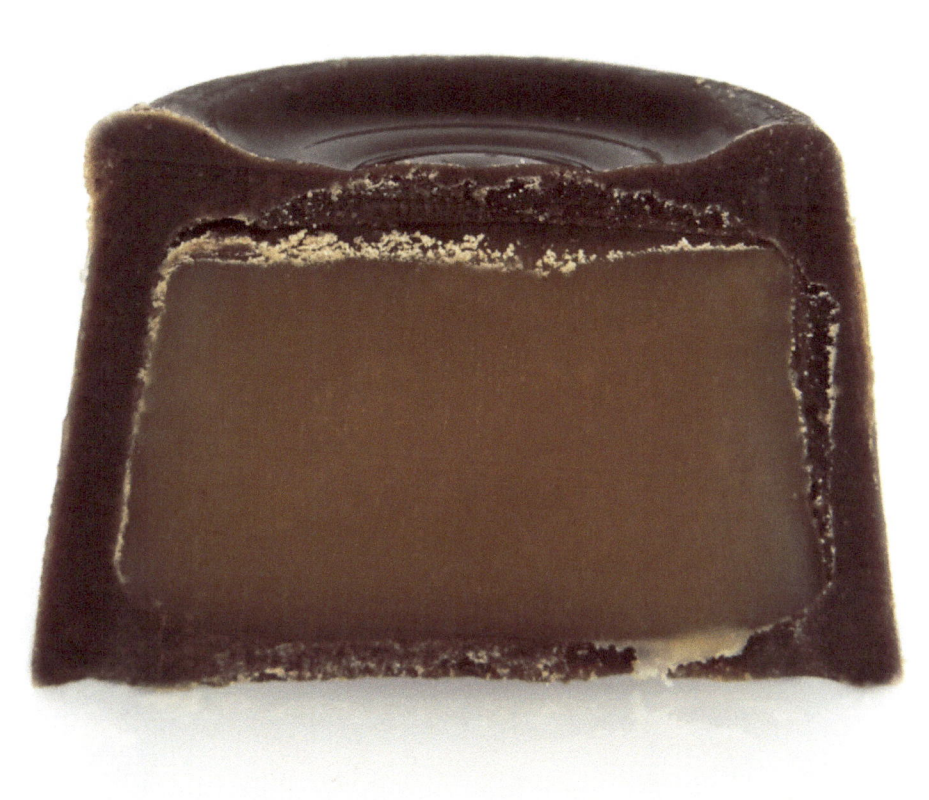

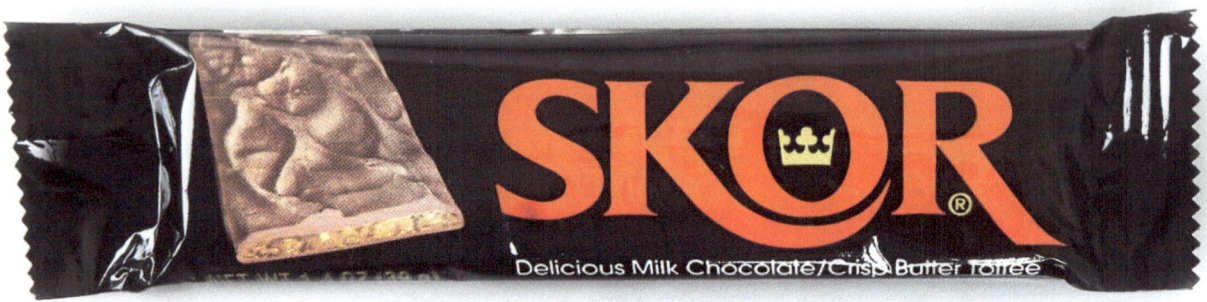

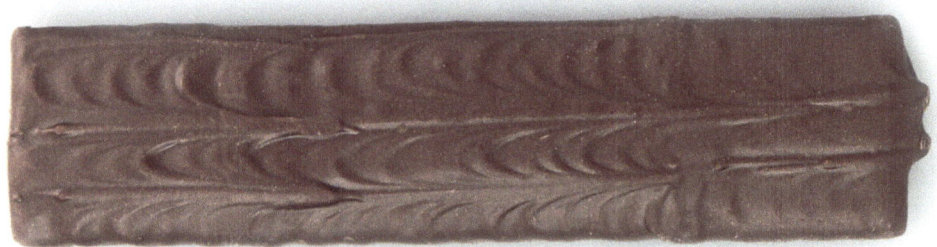

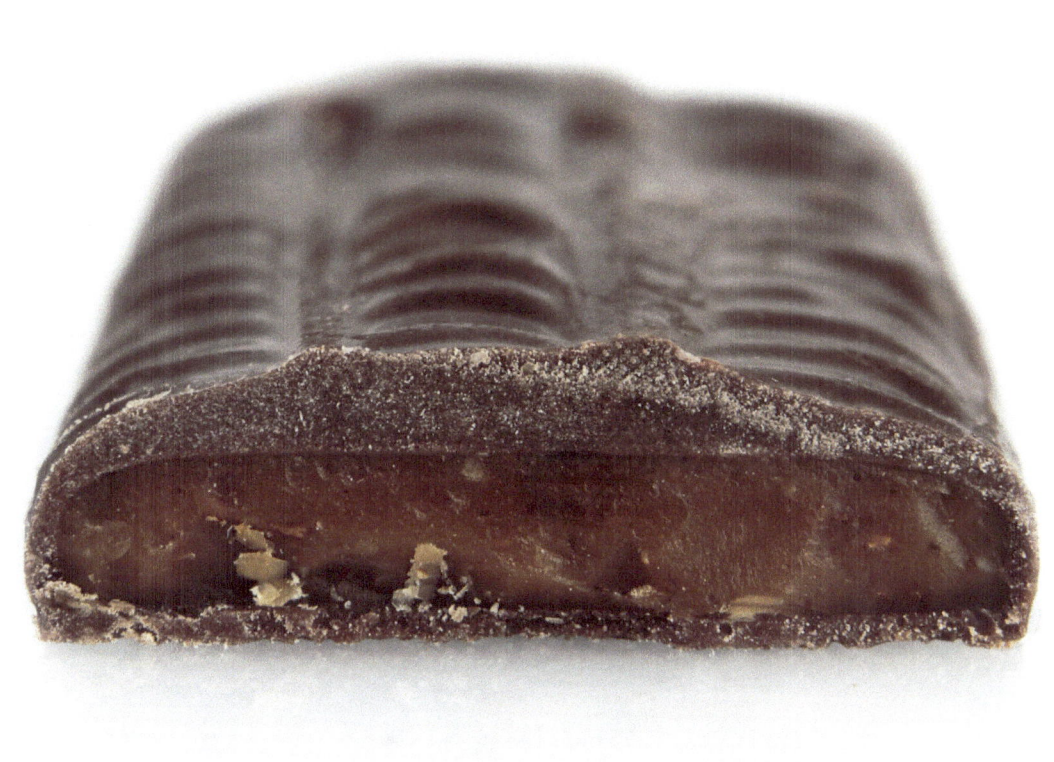

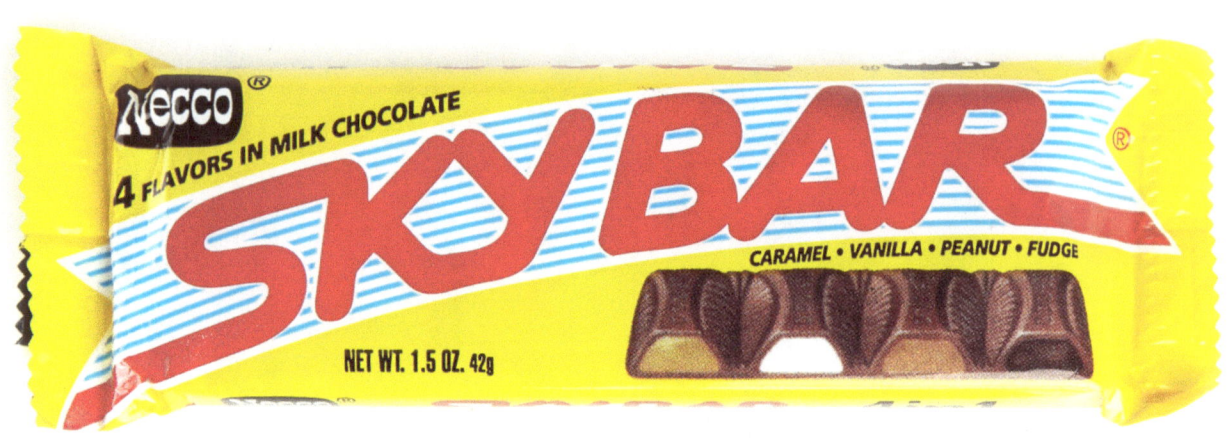

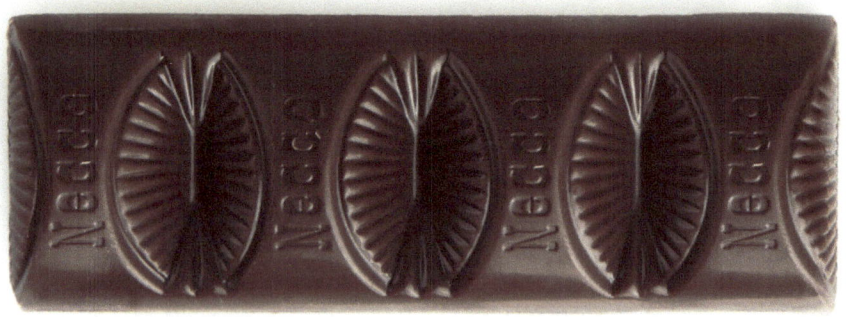

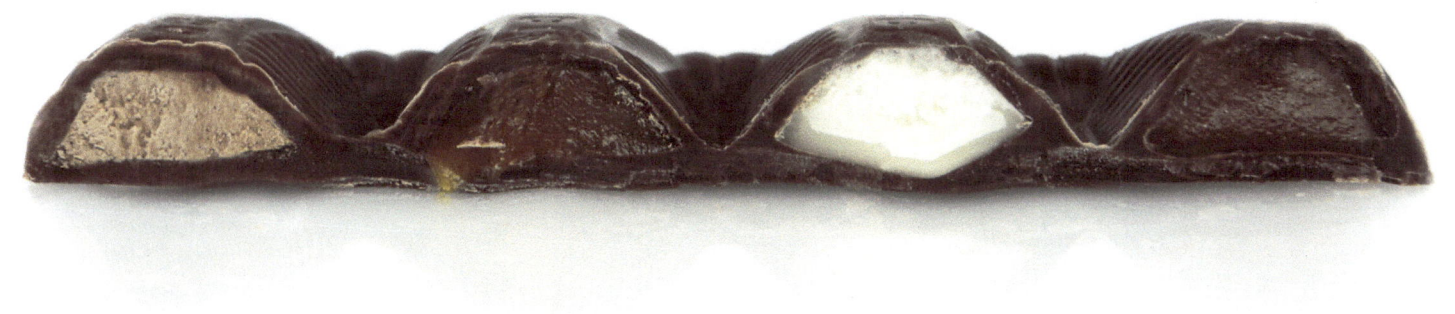

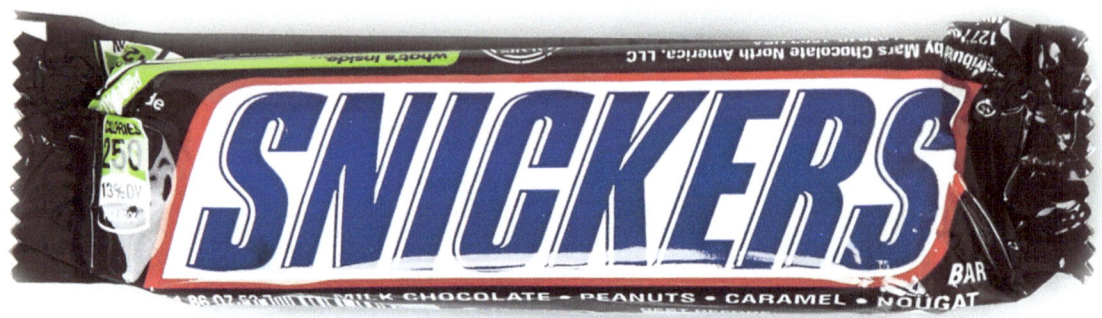

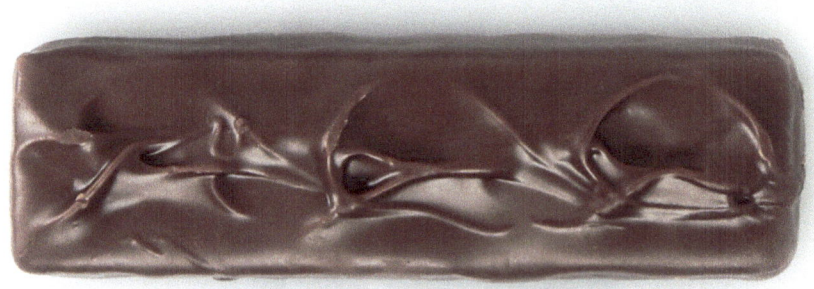

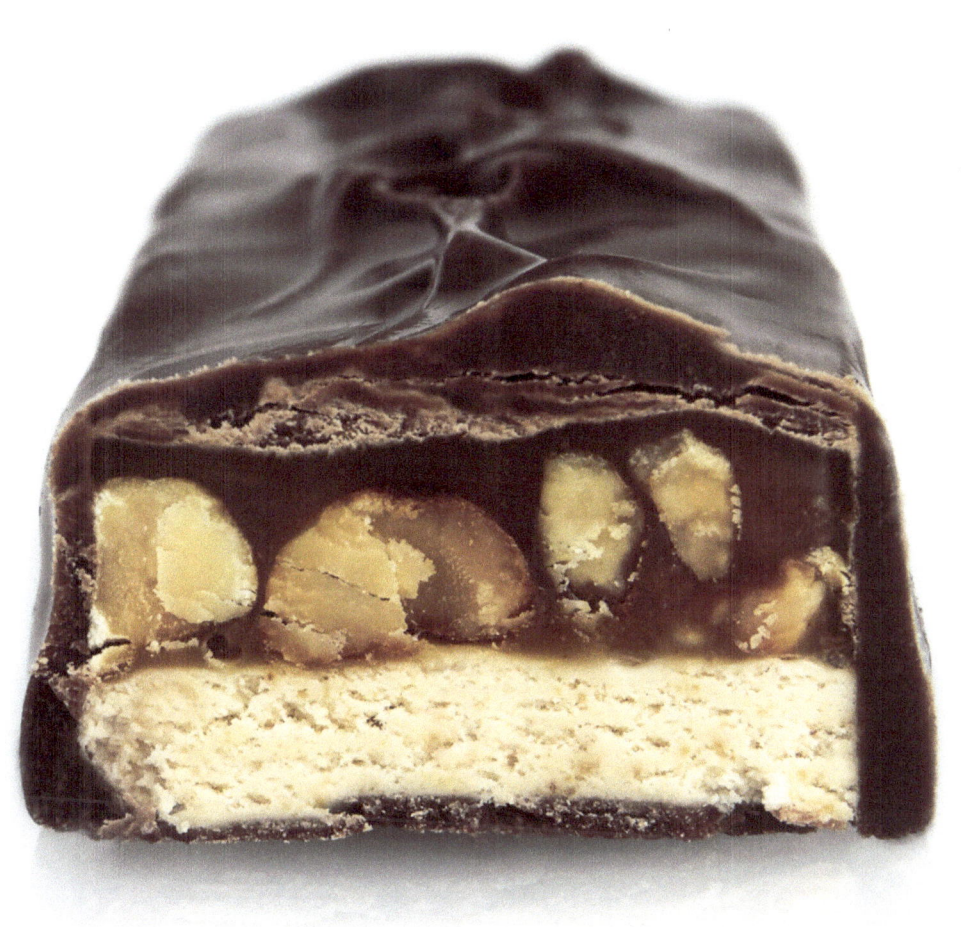

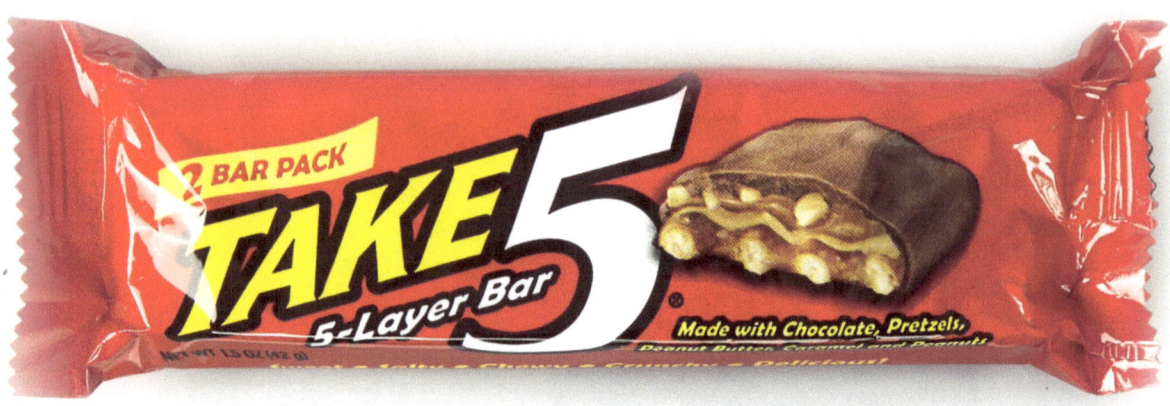

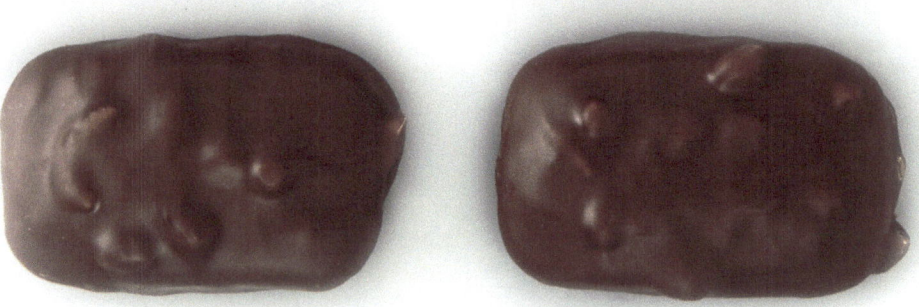

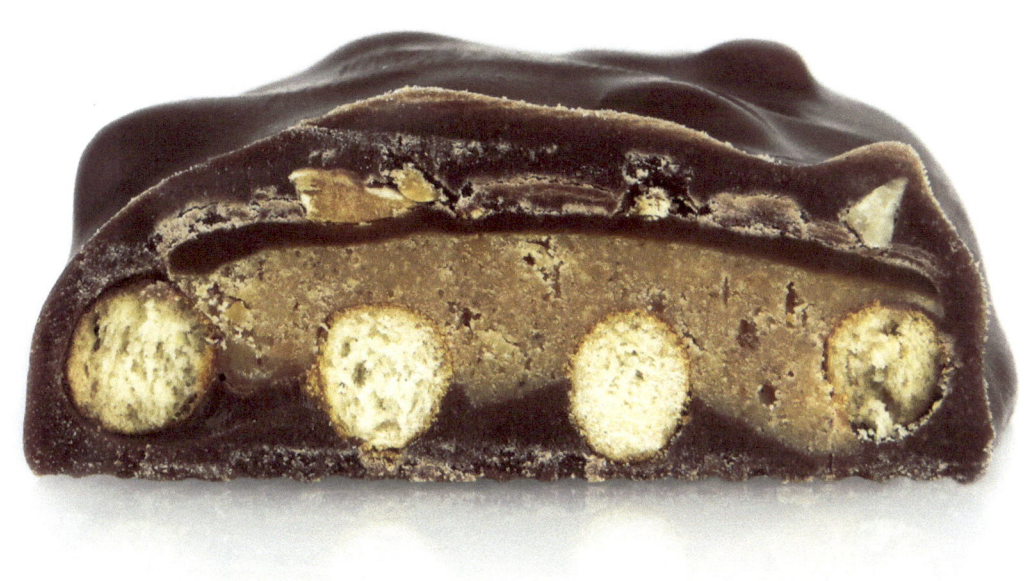

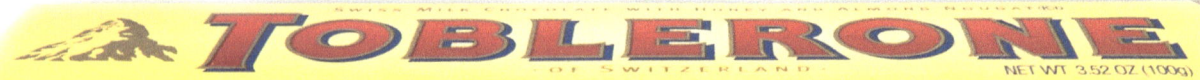

SWISS MILK CHOCOLATE WITH HONEY AND ALMOND NOUGAT ®

TOBLERONE

·OF SWITZERLAND· NET WT 3.52 OZ (100g)

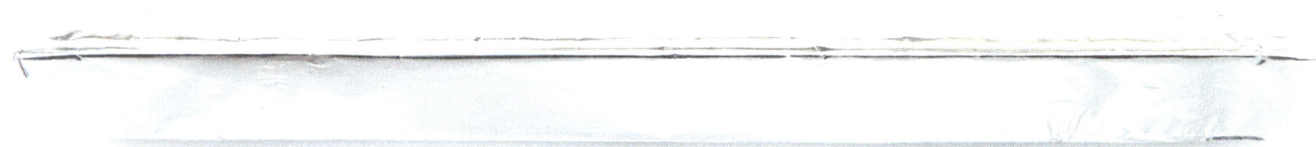

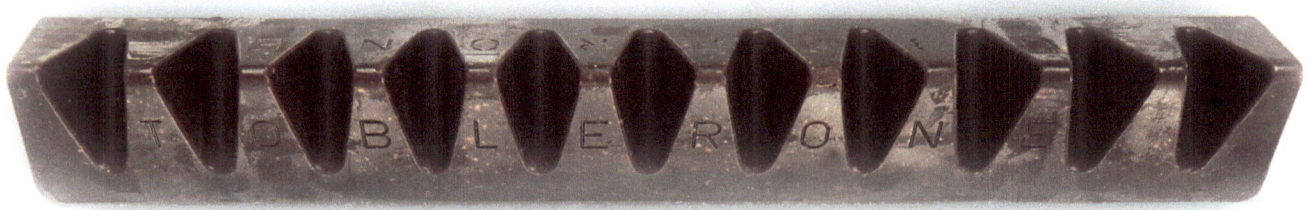

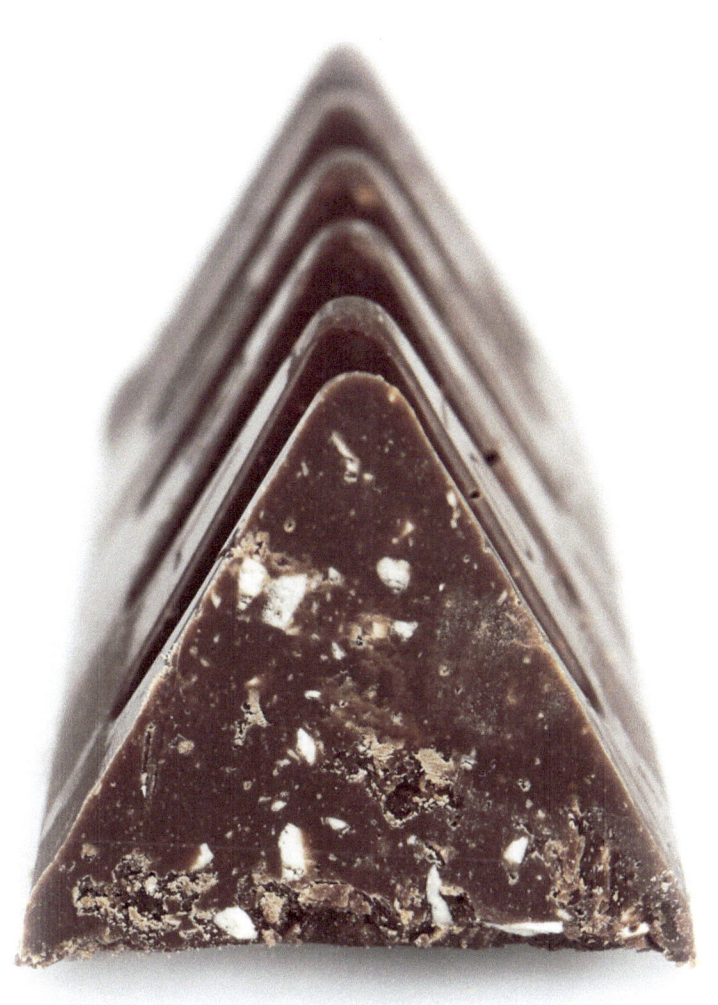

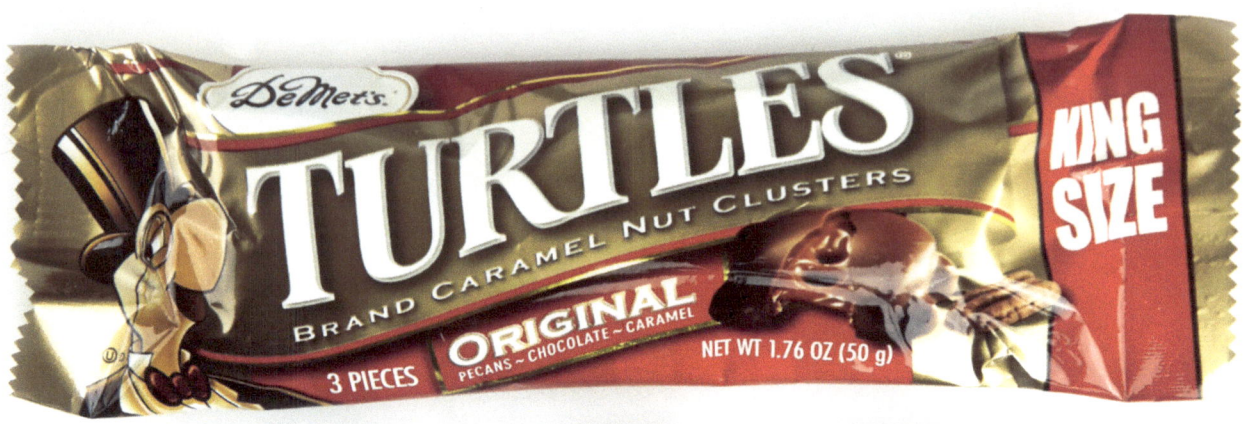

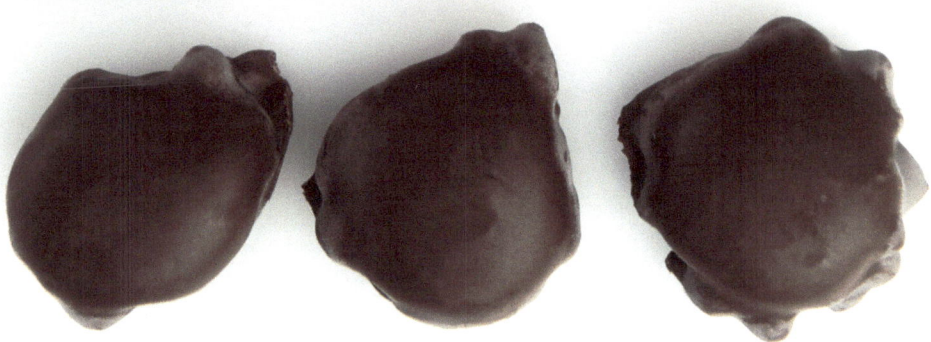

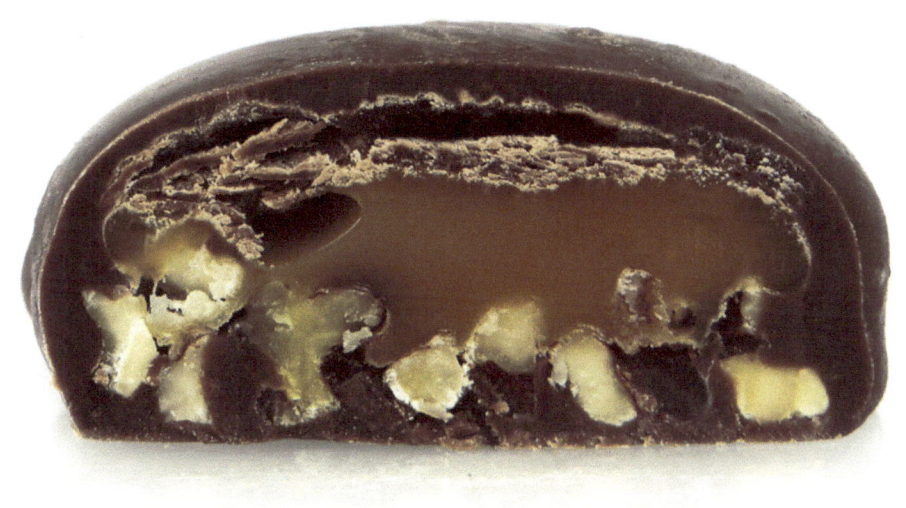

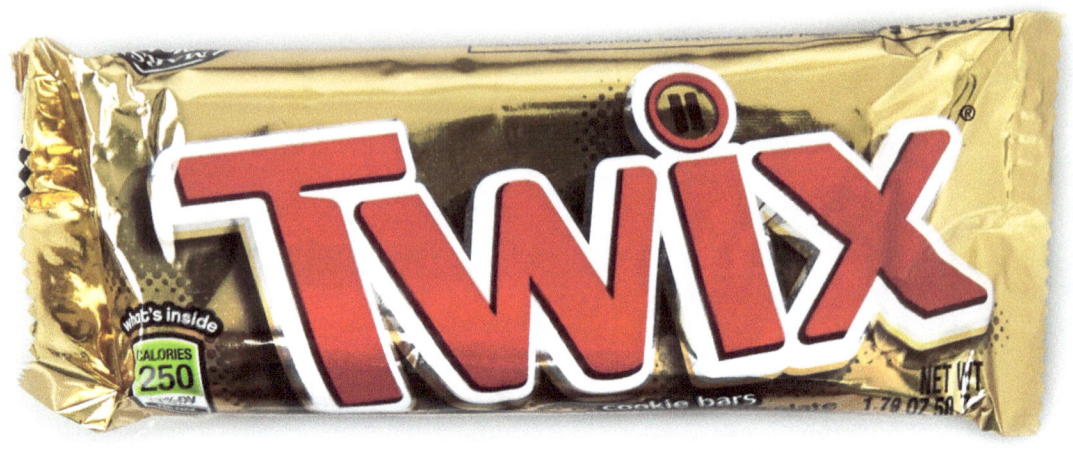

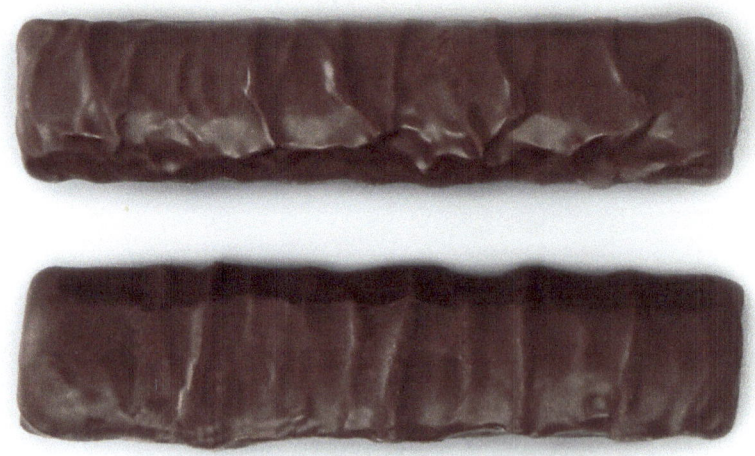

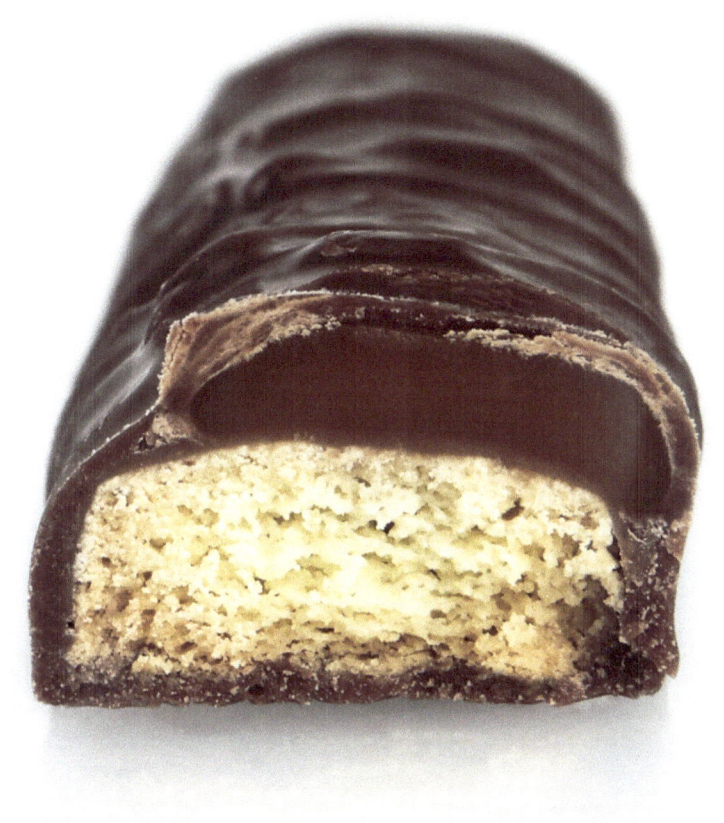

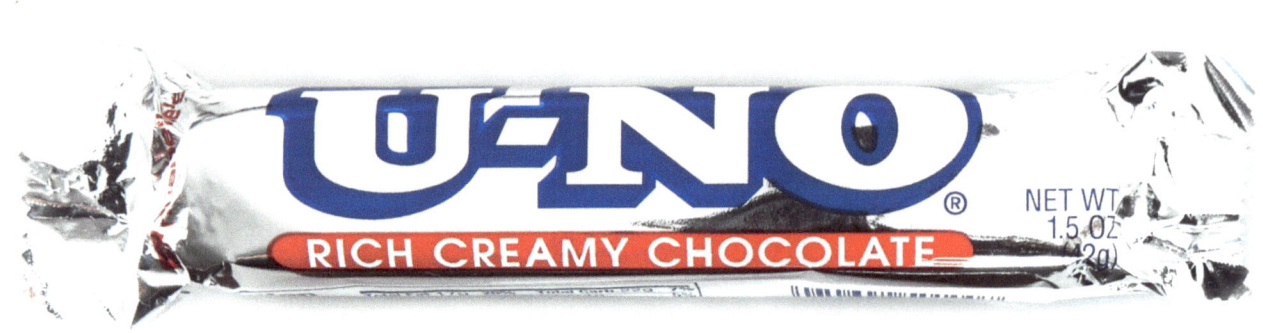

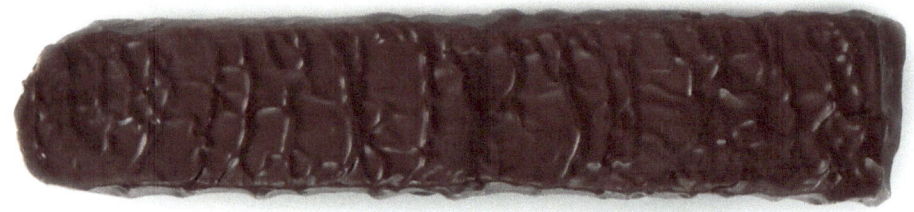

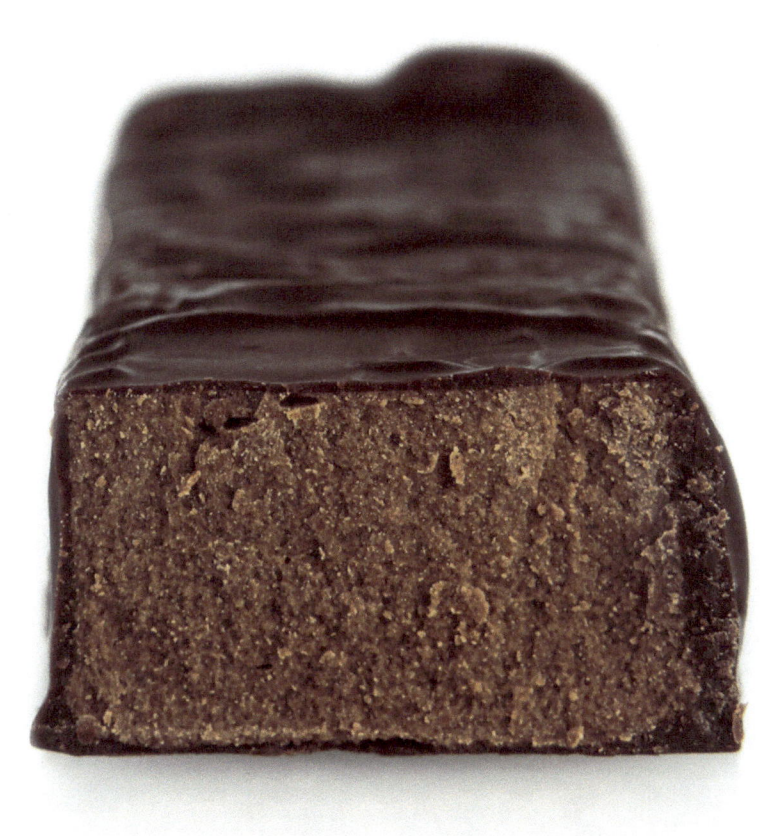

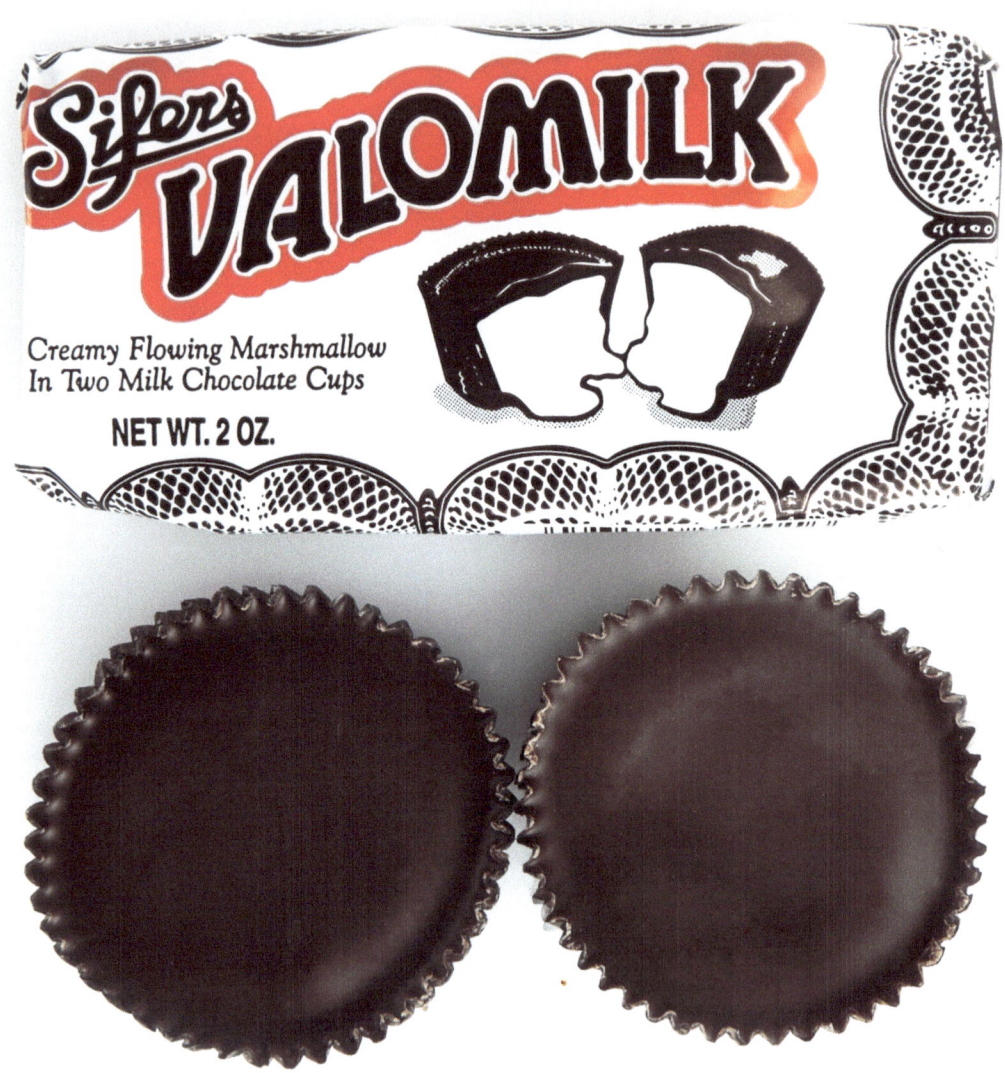

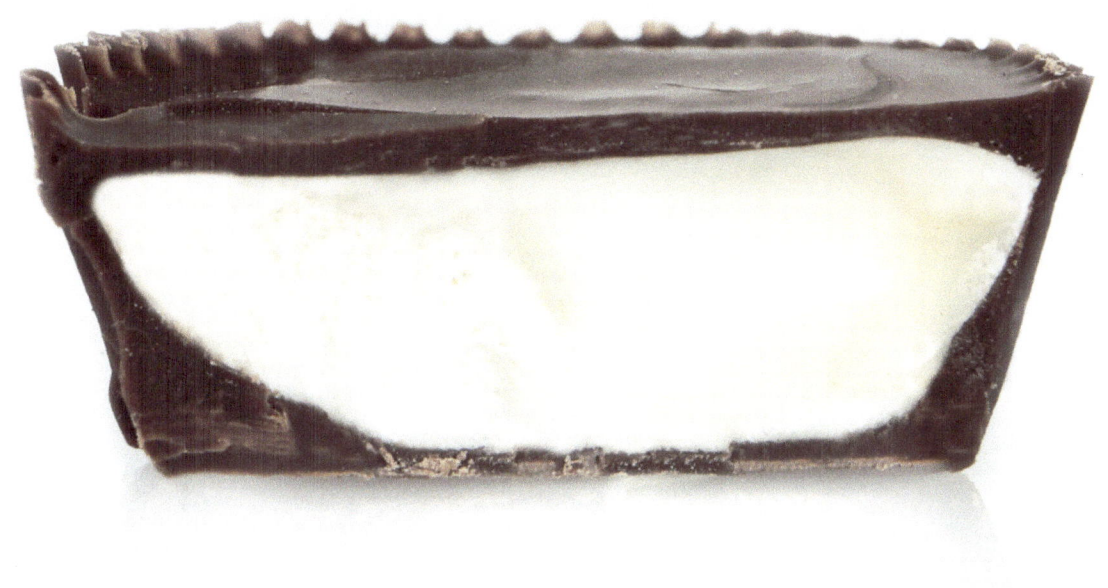

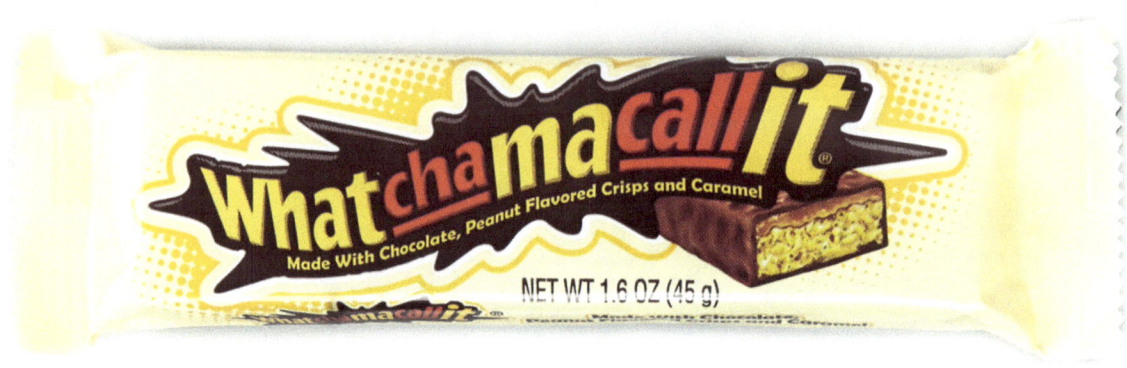

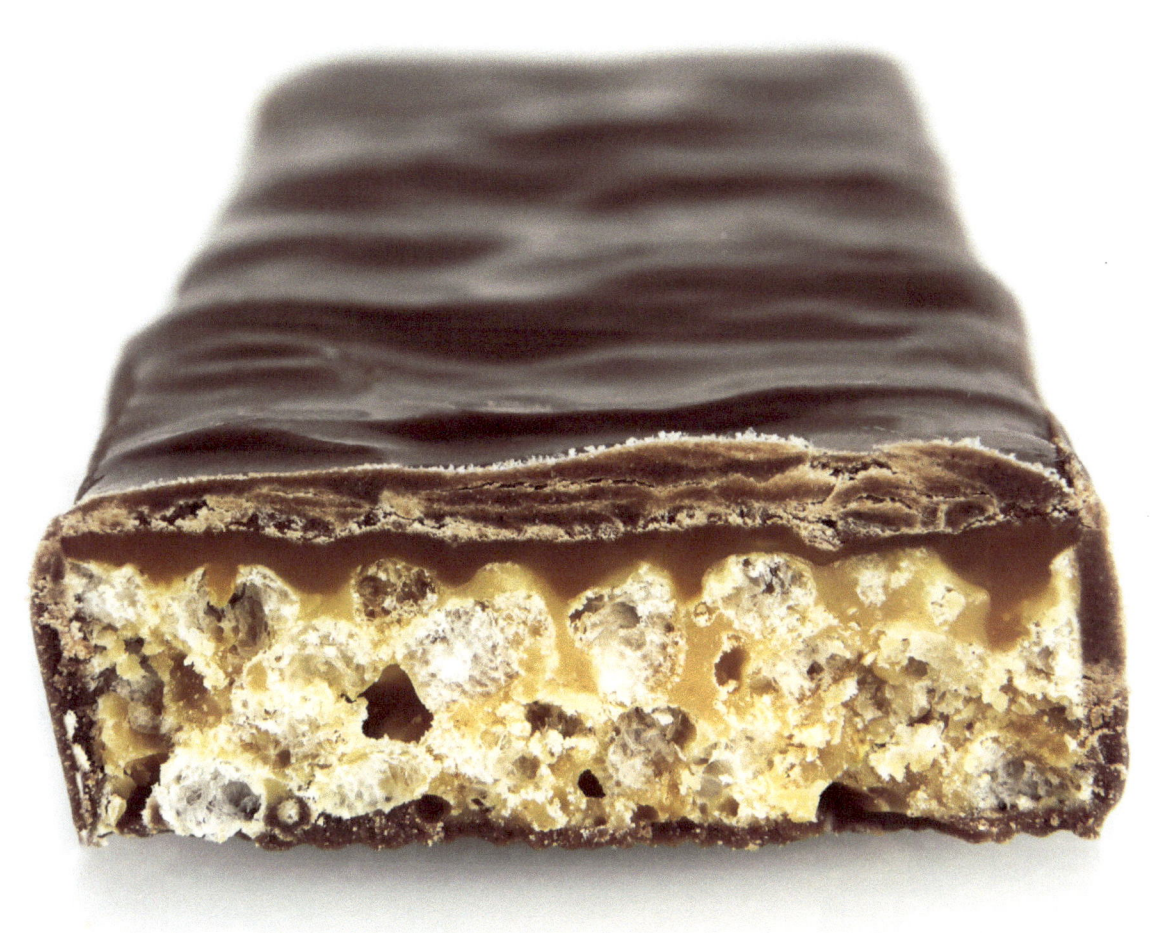

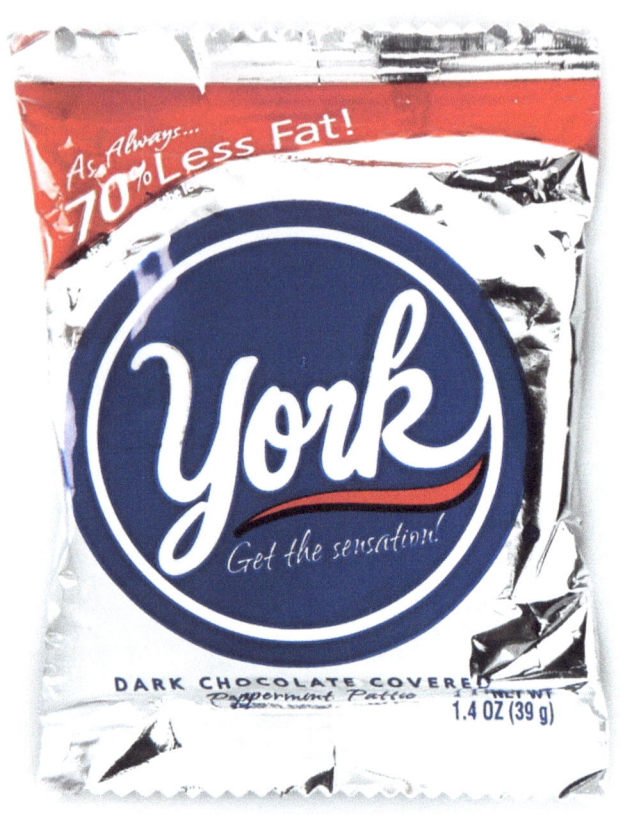

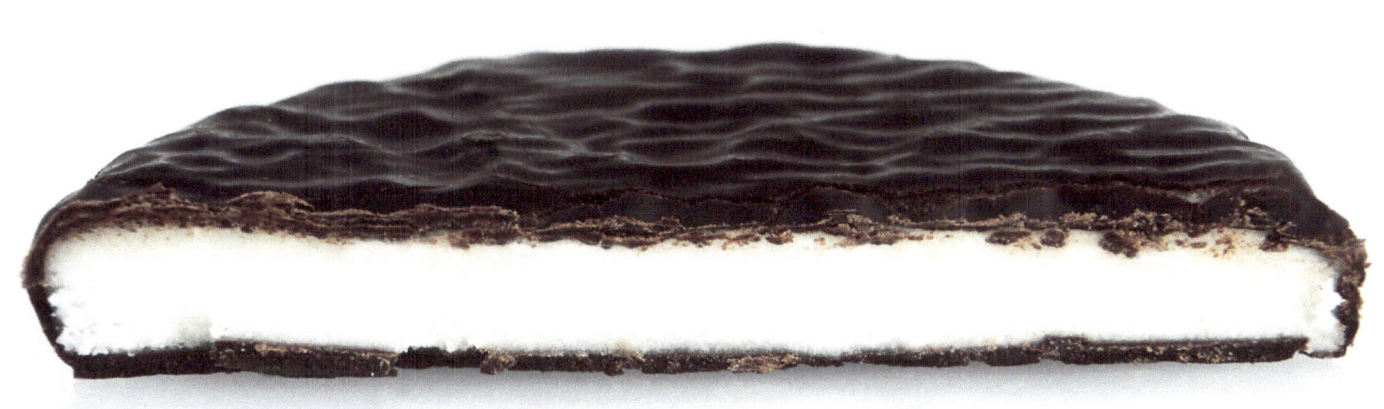

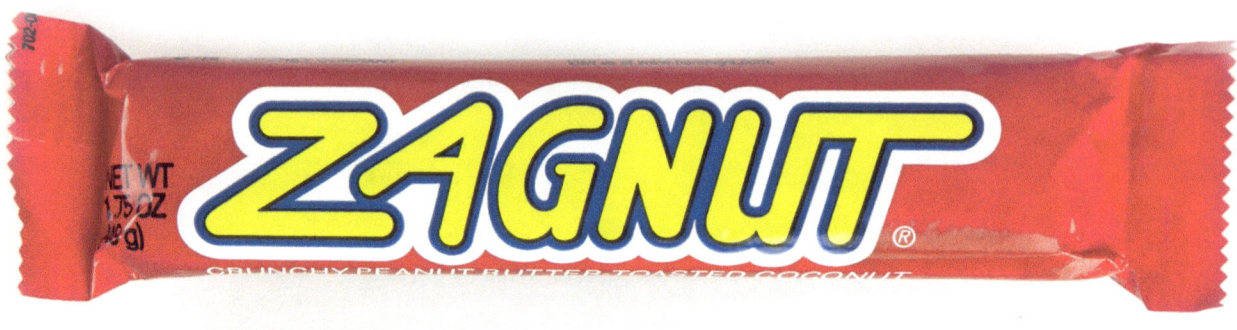

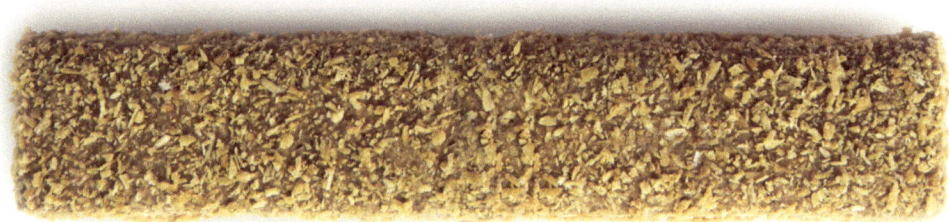

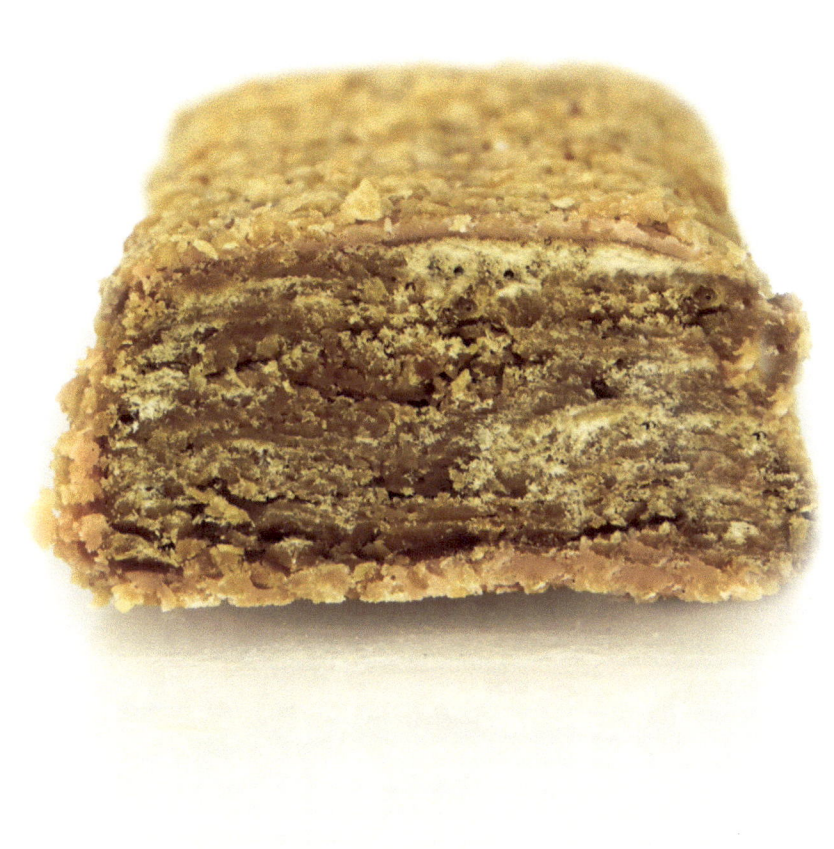

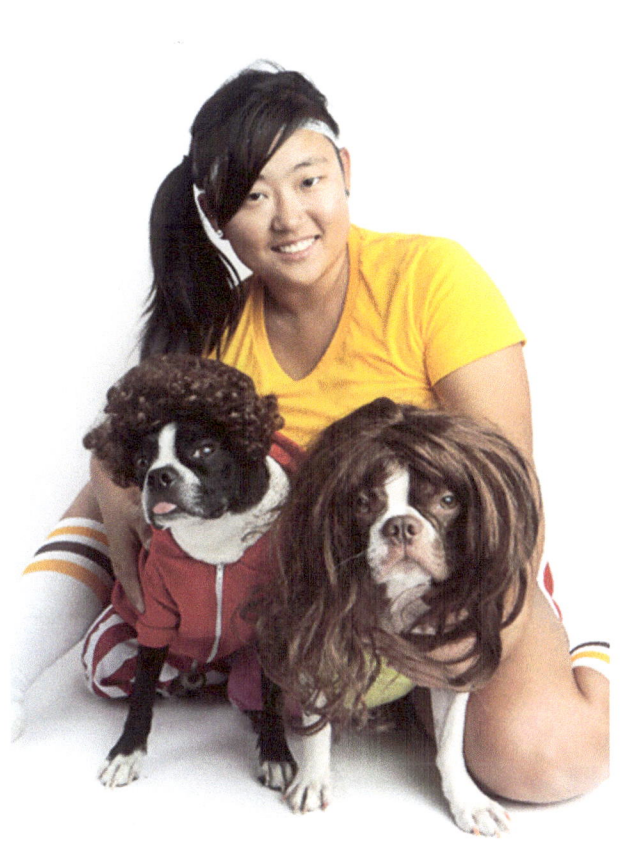

ABOUT KIRA STACKHOUSE

Kira Stackhouse is a native of Bethlehem, PA, currently living the dream in the San Francisco Bay Area as a photographer and entrepreneur. Her photos have appeared in many books and magazines nationwide.

Candy Barchive was created after Kira ate an obscene amount of Halloween candy in October 2013. She is pictured with her fur-kids Harley (as Richard Simmons) and Penelope (as Jane Fonda), both Boston terriers.

Kira's favorite candy bars are Snickers, Kit Kat and Goldenberg's Peanut Chews.

www.candybarchive.com

www.ingramcontent.com/pod-product-compliance
Lightning Source LLC
Chambersburg PA
CBHW050851180526
45159CB00007B/2640